Moments In HerStory

From Pain to Purpose: Testimonies of Young Girls

Second Edition

Moments in HerStory by Lakita Stewart-Thompson
Published by Through Words Publishing, LLC
Severn, MD
www. namaduw.org

Copyright © 2015 by Through Words Publishing, LLC

Scripture quotations marked (NLT) are taken from the Holy Bible. New Living Translation copyright © 1997. Used by permission of Tyndale House Publishers Inc. Wheaton, Illinois 60189. All rights reserved.

Scripture quotations marked (KJV) are taken from the Holy Bible. King James Version copyright © 1997. Used by permission of Tyndale House Publishers Inc. Wheaton, Illinois 60189. All rights reserved.

All real life stories are used with permission from actual parties involved and recorded to the best of the author's recollections.

All rights reserved solely by publisher. The publisher guarantees all contents are original and do not infringe upon the legal rights of any other person or work. No part of this publication may be reproduced, stored in retrieval system, or transmitted in any form or by any means, electronic, mechanical, photocopying, recording or otherwise without the prior permission of the publisher.

The publisher is not responsible for websites (or their content) mentioned in this book that are not owned by the publisher.

Cover by: Maxphotomaster

ISBN-13:
978-0692488676
ISBN-10:
0692488677
Printed in the United States

Dedication

I would like to dedicate this book to my Papa Mshairi Alkebular for always believing in me. I appreciate the positive words he always spoke into and over my life. He always told me that I was special and would become something in life. Also, to my Auntie and godmother, Selena Bradley (Lena) for always pushing me to do my best despite my life challenges. I will always cherish the many years of your encouragement and teachings.
I love you both and I know you would be proud.

Forever in my heart your Nuk and Mooky-Mook…

Acknowledgements

First to my Lord and Savior Jesus Christ for allowing this book to come to fruition and trusting me with the vision. I thank God for all his blessings and for allowing me this opportunity to share my story.

I would like to acknowledge the following:

My rock, my caregiver, my number one supporter, my Mother Minister Tanya L. Baylor. Without you I don't know what my life would be like. You are the piece that holds everything together. Mom, you are truly a blessing that can never be replaced.

My Pastor, Co-Pastor, and my Deliverance Headquarters for All People church family. I thank Pastor Al and Co-Pastor Sabrina Harris for always being there for me and loving me unconditionally. I appreciate you both for keeping me in continuous prayer while encouraging me through my ministry and life's journey. Pastor Al and Co-Pastor Sabrina I especially thank you for living and leading by example with such humility and obedience.

Mr. James Hillian Jr., aka "Mr. Star," for being a wonderful male inspiration in my life. I appreciate your valuable insight, guidance and contributions to my ministry. You are truly an anointed and appointed man of God.

My immediate family who loves and support me. I truly appreciate all of you and the many things you do, for it doesn't go unnoticed. I would like to thank my "village family" that has stepped in to help take care of me throughout the years. You all have played a special role in the young lady I am today.

To the contributing writers, thank you for your participation in this project. I thank you for sharing your stories and providing encouragement to help the lives of other young ladies and women overcome adversity. May God bless you for your willingness, boldness, obedience, and for being transparent.

To Ms. Kita Stewart-Thompson for being there to help make *"Moments in HerStory From Pain to Purpose: Testimonies of Young Girls."* happen. You have truly dedicated yourself by sacrificing your time and finances to help me accomplish this goal. You have been working diligently from the day I expressed my vision to you. You held me accountable and taught me that I can do whatever my heart desires. Auntie Kita without you I don't believe this book and the goal would have been accomplished. Thank you for always supporting me, my ministry, and working with me to make my vision become a reality.

May they continue to rest in peace my late Auntie Selena (Lena) and Papa Mshairi. I know that they would be proud of the young lady that I have become. If it wasn't for their help, teachings, encouragement, and discipline I don't know where or what I would be. Papa showed me the importance of reading and writing as he introduced me to the art of African Soul. He shared his knowledge and believed in me. My Auntie Lena was just my heart in human form as she will always be. She was a woman that is un-describable and words simply cannot express how much she loved me and I loved her. She was very understanding and always had my back protecting me against anything and anyone. My Papa and Auntie Lena mean the world to me and I would do anything to see them again. I love you both and I know you are in a better place because God loved you more.
Until we meet again….

Contents

Foreword 7
Introduction 8
Used to Be Abused 11
I'm Not Perfect But I'm Worth It 40
Learning to Live Without You 57
It's Not Unto Death 87
Let's Talk About Sex 101
Why Daddy 125
You're Expected to Win 142
Index 169
Resources 172

Foreword

A lot of times I think about whom I would be if I did have my father around and I honestly don't think I want to know. I like who I turned out to be. I like the fact that I had to struggle to get to where I am. I like the fact that I had to endure some hurt and pain because now I am stronger because of it.

I often hear people say that girls who have grown up without a father figure will gravitate towards guys because they are in search of that love they never got. I was in search of that type of love but at the same time I knew that everyone couldn't give that genuine love that a father can give. I am very adamant about who I let love me or who I give my heart to and a lot of people say that's a bad thing but I really disagree.

Growing up without a father, being raped at an early age; molested for years; and then becoming a single teenage Mom raising 3 children wasn't the plan I had for my life. However, by the grace of God I nurtured my children who are now all independent young adults; I've maintained a full time government job for 29 years and now married for 4 years. It hasn't been easy but it's all been worth it. The heartache, headaches and hardships have all made me into the woman that I am today. Just know my story isn't your story and we all may have a different endings based on what God chooses for us to endure as good soldiers. Be encouraged knowing that he who begun a good work in you will complete it. So as you read the testimonies of these young ladies know that God has a plan for their lives too. No matter what it looks like know God has the final say.

His Servant,

Reverend Robin Anderson

Introduction

Dear Baby Girl,

    From the moment I realized you were conceived I knew that you were special. I never knew the reason why but now I know your purpose could not be aborted. Although I may have endured many months of heartache, sickness, and loneliness ultimately the pain produced purpose.

    From conception the late Reverend Beauty D. Hines anointed hands were laid, life of greatness was spoken, and endless prophesies were given that are manifesting until this day. As I watched you triumph over the many tribulations since a young child I vast in the glory of how the God in you has overcome the barriers that was set before you.

    You could have never counted up the cost for your life's journey because the anointing and call upon your life was pre-destined. Through your spiritual nurturing you have acquired a heart of a servant which has birthed a creative passion to live a life that is pleasing unto God.

    As we embark upon the paths of young ladies and women who have experienced similar adversities we learn that our pain ignites the strength within to walk in our God given purpose.

Love always,

Mommy
Minister Tanya L. Baylor

We Are Not Different We Are the Same

Charmaine Betty-Singleton

Although you are in another county state or country
Standing on different land
Your struggles trials and tribulations
I promise you I understand
I have problems with bullying fighting and also have been called out my name
But sitting here reading your testimony
We are not different we are the same
You don't like school and homework and get mad at your mother too
You may live in a shelter have no food surrounded by drugs and don't know what to do
Boys and men look at you like an appetizer and try to cop a feel when you pass by
You feel lonely abandoned depressed and unworthy and you cry and you cry and you cry
You look in the mirror in disgust because you don't like what you see
Because some hateful and bitter soul convinced you that you are not pretty
You reached out to the wrong person to find love and had sex without using a condom
Now you worried scared out of your mind
Wandering, if you will have a daughter or son
You try so hard to study pass all tests to be a success in school
But your parents tell you that they don't have any money for college and you are feeling like a fool
You don't like how you are feeling
you don't like girly things and feel strange inside
You wear oversized clothes and Tims
wondering if you are a girl or a guy

Well my sister these are issues
We all face every day all over world
This is the plight the journey we take because we were all born girls
Thank you for sharing your testimony and maybe we can bridge the gap
I promise to pray for you if you pray for me and through it all I have your back
Our testimonies bind us together from now to eternity
We are not different we are the same because I am you and you are me
Sharing moments in our story

Dedicated to our young girls all over the world!

~Used to Be Abused~

For I reckon that the sufferings of this present time are not worthy to be compared with the glory which shall be revealed in us.
Romans 8:18 KJV

Mended by His Grace
Ariel Mitchell

    I can remember a dark place. A place I went to very often, one that I eventually resided in. This place was not a physical location in-fact I moved around so much as a foster child that I was too afraid to consider a physical location home. This place was a constant mental state of fear, sadness, and hopelessness.

    My days early on in life had never been certain. One day I could be safe in my early foster homes where I was unhappy, but knew no detrimental harm…other days I would fear and fight for my life. Those days would be filled with 'games' that my father's wife at the time would use to torment me out of pure hatred.

    Not many seven year olds can say they have conditioned themselves to not only read people but, also learned to use those skills to protect themselves and their father. Those skills did not exactly protect me or my father but, taking the blows meant she would get it out of her system and maybe *just maybe* she would leave my dad alone.

    Bruises, broken noses, scars, and random ER visits were normal to me. I call the visits to the hospital random because after a while, I got used to living in a constant state of pain, or soreness from the constant blows my body took from her rage…so being woken up in the middle of the night to 'visit the doctor' again was routine for me.

    As years passed, my hope diminished. With every home or move, came a new type of abuse or betrayal. I became the quiet, introverted, anxious little girl that predators like my foster father took advantage of. The kind of girl who was bullied and preferred mean kids at school, rather than the nightmares at home. When someone raised their voice I shook uncontrollably, when I was 'prey' to someone who was entrusted to care for me. I began to calculate time-to the minute of when he would leave for work. I even memorized the sounds of footsteps so that I would always be aware of who was approaching.

Things got better when I moved again before high school. It was different with this placement. My foster mom treated me like a long lost daughter, her sons called me sister, and I was able to do things like walk into the kitchen without getting yelled at...I felt happy and safe at last. In hopes of maintaining the idea of being someone's 'daughter', I ignored the signs when things began to change. I was adopted by sixteen, but the 'good times' would grow gradually apart. By eighteen I was a full-fledged house servant. No longer called by my name, I was officially 'her'.

After a year and a half of maintaining a household, cooking, cleaning, becoming a caretaker, working full time, and going to school full time, I not only watched my hope fade away, but I watched my self-worth fade away too.

It's been over two years since my escape. The escape was not easy. I lived in shelters for months I walked miles in frigid cold weather afraid for my life, nearly died from starvation and dehydration, and was tormented and stalked for the first year and a half by my so-called 'mom'. I would not have survived ONE NIGHT of that nightmare if it were not for the people that God placed in my life from the day I decided to leave. HE rescued me and used God fearing, compassionate individuals as His vessels to protect and guide me.

Some call me a survivor, others see me as an 'inspiration'...I am neither one. I define myself as a daughter of the King. I thrive because of Him, because He had bigger plans for me. I am alive because of His GRACE. My relationship with the Lord is one that grows every day. My love and passion to grow closer to God is infinite. It is through Him that we are saved, and nothing can tear me away from my Father in Heaven because I am a sinner who is CHOSEN, LOVED, I was a nobody, and God picked me up and said, "No, you are MY daughter and you will be a vessel for My glory."

I do not volunteer because I feel I owe anyone anything. God has blessed me with a servant's heart because we are all called to shine our lights for Him and to be vessels for Him. He uses what we have been through for GOOD. Why call ourselves 'courageous' if we don't use our experiences to bring someone else closer to God?

I was abused, but I'm not ashamed because the rape, the mental and physical abuse eventually led me back to the Lord and because of His grace, I choose to dedicate my life to serving His children. I cannot be ashamed to proclaim the truth, let alone the story that our Creator has written on my heart. His gospel was meant to be shared, and I pray that my testimony not only displays heartbreak and tribulation, but God's amazing love for us.

The Stranger That I Know...
NaKyiah K. Nichols

For two and half years of my life I was showered with gifts, clothing, shoes, love and always going out to eat at restaurants. This man was daddy and mommy's boyfriend. For those two and half years I was a 5 year old living it up. I was living the dream life, mom got a man and I got a father figure and we both got love until that day when my mom cooked dinner that I refused to eat because I wanted "Popeye's." My mom told me, "You better call him because I'm not going to get Popeye's and I just cooked." So of course I did call him and he bought me my food. As my mother was in the kitchen I ate my food and me and my father figure sat, talked, laughed and joked around. However, the telephone rang, and as a normal child I picked up the phone and said, "Hello." It just so happen to be an old male friend of my mom who was calling to check on her. So I handed the telephone to my mom and told that man (I knew who soon would become a stranger) and said, "My mommy going to have a new boyfriend and you're not going to be her boyfriend anymore." At that moment my mommy told me to shut my mouth. I soon realized the look on this man face was so furious as if he was going to kill someone. I immediately became scared because of how he was staring at my mommy. My mom looked at him as if she knew what was going to happen next. I sat back and kept eating my dinner then he begins to ask my mother questions that she refused to answer. The next thing I knew is he picked up a glass and threw it at my mom's face but by the grace of God it missed her face by an inch. I immediately, stood up and begin to cry as I ran over to where my mother was. I cried thinking that this situation and he being angry was all my fault. If only I would have shut my mouth or not answered the telephone everything would have been okay. He started to walk towards me and my mother with his blood shot red eyes, and his veins where coming through his head and arms. His fist was balled up tight

and the pace he was walking was slow. I remember hearing my mother saying something like, "Oh Lord not again." As I looked up he had hit my mother. My mother begins to fight back. The next thing I knew I was forcefully being shoved into my room by him. While sitting in my room I could hear him and my mother still arguing and fighting. I tried to come out of my room, screaming and fighting this man saying,
"Get off my mommy!"
"Let go of her!"
"Stop!"
"Stop!"
Of course hitting him and screaming didn't work; he would just push me off him and kept fighting my mom. It wasn't until I stood in between him and my mother that he had pushed me into the wall. To me I was hurt, angry and full of rage. This was a part of him I've never seen before! I felt like I didn't know who this man was. I trusted him and he fights my mother. He soon became a stranger. He beat, tortured, and hurt my mom for hours. This lasted a really long time all throughout the night until the morning. My mother was basically fighting for her life. I was mad, sad, angry and felt like he betrayed us by his actions and I couldn't believe it. I cried as he called my mother everything but a child of God! My mom tried calling the police but he struck her every time she would pick up the telephone. Even though my mother fought back he continued to beat her. I was disturbed by his actions. Nevertheless, the police came and took a report and told my mom what actions to take. My mom sat me down and we had a long talk about everything that had happened that night. Everything was okay because I begin to go to counseling and recover from my mental hurt. I thought it was all over until the stalking began. He would sit outside of the house, my mother's job and our church home. I could not believe it! This man who was nice to me and took care of me was now what I would call a creep. He would show up at our house and threw rocks at the window calling our name and cursing. I became very scared of him but knew I had to see who was now a stranger at church the place I have to go to every Sunday. I don't know what happened in court (because my mom filed charges against him) but I do know our

house telephone rung 24/7 and he continually texted my mother. Eventually, as time went on the pop-up visits, telephone calls, and text stopped. I was glad that he was finally out of our lives.

At this point I was a 5 year old who couldn't really hold a grudge. As time went on and I became older my mom would periodically have conversations with me on how a man is supposed to treat a woman. She would explain to me on how to understand my worth and that God didn't create us to be abused but to be loved. I would tell myself that I couldn't hold grudges and I would pray and ask God to heal me from the hurt, anger and pain I was feeling. One day it happened, I finally forgave this stranger and started back loving him again. I can honestly say that I forgave this man. Now I attend the same church as this man and I can say genially love him. I'm able to hug him, laugh with him and praise God with him.

In the past I wasn't optimistic about the future, but God gave me a change of heart towards the stranger I knew. This was a blessing for me. I have learned that in order to live a happy and healthy life we have to forgive. If I can encourage anyone reading this book, I would say forgive and forget. Life is too short to have a heavy hurting heart. So please, let go and let God have his way and try to have a renewed heart, spirit, and mind. Be Blessed!

No More Pain

Rene Michelle

It wasn't the first time and I prayed it would never happen again. I had already suffered enough. My life just seemed like one big ball of hurt. I felt like if I could get past the last situation and come out alive nothing else could faze me. I promised myself I would never let a man hurt me again. Then I met him! He was so handsome all of my girlfriends were putting in bids and just gawking him. We were at a friend's Mother's funeral and I noticed him but was not really moved like them although he was quite handsome. After the funeral our eyes met as I was leaving the ladies room. He struck up a conversation and at that point we begin a friendship that lead to a really speedy relationship. The relationship grew really fast. He was very caring and giving at least in the beginning he was. As time went on I noticed his attitude changing. I also noticed he was drinking really heavily. With the drinking his attitude was so different. He would say mean things and become rather aggressive. I tried to overlook the drinking because it wasn't often that he did it.

As time went on he eventually started staying at my house regularly. He began doing things that were very disrespectful like coming in late, smelling of a woman's perfume. At some point I felt I no longer needed or was interested in him or his mess. It started to show. I wasn't attentive as I was before. I really just wanted him to leave. This one night he asked me to go to a party with him and I told him no, I wanted to stay home and rest. It was obvious I was losing interest. I was always with him when I had free time. That changed tremendously. He went to the party without me. The evening went on before I knew it the time was four o'clock am. I hear a knock on the door and I come down the steps very disturbed needless to say, I open the door and it's him with his brother and sister- n-law. He reeked of alcohol. Lord only knows what else. Not trying to be rude I sat downstairs with them until they decided to finally leave. At that point I'm tired frustrated just livid, I decided to go back upstairs to bed. He had other plans. As I walked up the steps he called me back. I realize when he walked in he had a large trash bag with an object in it. Although I really didn't want to I came back down to find out what he wanted. He then pulled out a double barrel shot gun from the trash bag and began pointing it at me. In mind I'm saying oh no Lord help me not again! I had already been down this road before with a previous relationship. I couldn't believe this was happening again. I kindly asked him to please stop pointing the gun at me and put it away. I said, "Why did you bring that here knowing how I feel about guns? I don't like them!" He refused to put it away. He began to fight me and somehow we ended up on the couch. I'm crying and screaming because by this time he has me in a choke hold as he's choking me he's pushing my head down into the crease of the couch. I'm screaming for my life and gasping for air. Then there's a knock at the door, I heard!!! Open the door it's the Police! He jumps up and tells me to get it but I better not say anything. He runs upstairs to hide. I opened the door still disheveled, hair all over my head, tears still in my eyes reeking of urine from the choke hold he had on me, which caused me to lose control of my bladder. The Officers say to me, "Ma'am is everything ok? We got a call to this address saying that there was a young lady screaming for her life. Also, that a gun was involved. Is someone here with you?" They asked! I shook my head yes. They said, "were is he?" I pointed up the steps. They asked, "where's the gun?" I pointed upstairs. They asked my permission to go up the steps. I said, yes. They go up and then come down the steps with him and the gun. They asked him for identification. He couldn't produce one so they said they were taking him in until he could prove who he was and be sure he doesn't have warrants. They took him out in handcuffs. I'm shaken in disbelief. I decided to leave I was just afraid to be there. I thought they may release him and he would come back. Still with my body wreaking of urine my hair all over my head and my mind racing a thousand miles per minute. I left and drove to my brother's house. I get there and never got out of the car. I dozed off in my car. I was awakened by a loud bang on my window. I wake up to see my brother standing there wanting to know why I was outside his house sleep and asked what's wrong? He tells me to come in the house. Although I was hesitant I went in and at the time my oldest brother was living there as well. So, my brother calls my other brothers and they come and they all question me about what happened. After I explained to them, they all were ready to go looking for him. Throughout everything we've all seen and our painful past, I had never seen my oldest brother cry. He told me never to let a man think its okay to hit you. You have brothers! They were looking for him but I thank the good Lord they never ran into him because as always I was thinking about everyone else. I didn't want them to end up in jail. Needless to say that relationship was over. To God be the Glory!

      I'm no longer a victim! I'm a Survivor! If you are in an abusive relationship please leave! It doesn't get better. It will only get worse with time!

Why I stayed; then I ran!
Torri Rodgers-Ball

Domestic Violence comes in many different forms of abuse; Physical, Sexual, Mental, Verbal, and Economic Abuse. As the victim or survivor you are not at fault for someone else's behavior. If you or someone you know are involved in a situation as such; please have a safety plan with an exit strategy and/or call 911.

    At the age of 18, I thought I knew it all and almost had it all. After my break-up with my high school sweetheart; I met (what I thought) was a man. The man was 7 to 8 years my senior, whom I met at work during my lunch hour. At about 18 or 19; I smelled myself, as all teens do around that age. I had a good job, a car, single woman with no children, and attending college. As time went on, we dated and I just thought I was in love and decided against my parents' wishes and moved out in an apartment with this man that I thought I knew! (Key phrase), "Thought I Knew." As our lives went on together I became more involved with things that grabbed my attention to grow up and grow faster. I was pregnant! I was so terrified to tell my parents at the age of 19, that I was having a child. The only thing that was working on behalf was being a high school graduate and working full-time. The bad thing, the man I thought loved me told me to get an abortion.
    Terrified of being pregnant; I was absolutely terrified of having an abortion. So, I went with carrying my child and living with this man on and off. As life grew and I was getting into mommy mode, the abuse started too. The arguing, pushing, and name calling continued. As time went on, the rent money was taken from time to time to settle his gambling debts and I was no longer able to keep up with our rent. We left one place and lived in two separate households to live different lifestyles; me at home with my parents and he to live and date other women. While this was occurring, I would mask my pain with

smiles and a jovial attitude and go along to get along and eventually moved back into the apartment with him. The night before his father and stepmother were due to visit; we got into a physical altercation which resulted into a punch to the face and a slam to the floor with a six month exposed pregnant belly. I hide my black eye and avoided visits with my parents. After so much disrespect, I left the second time and went back home to be with my parents and to finish school.

After several years past; we decided to work towards a third try with a relationship to raise our child in a two parent household; we decided to live together again. As I grew older and my responsibilities grew; I became more daring and unbothered by my risky decisions in life. One year after my child was born; I decided to introduce my soul and temple to dancing. Once my decision was expressed to him; I was introduced to a woman that led me to the other side of my path. With no compliant from him because of the benefits; I went to try out drunk and was hired and working the same night. My physical look changed over time with clothing, make-up, and plenty of funds to match. After being involved with this lifestyle for a while; my confidence was becoming more defined and I realized that I could NOT serve two GODS ever. I decided to leave that lifestyle and focus on my child and myself.

After realizing that my daughter's father was not in love with me and his family; I left for good and started to look for my own home. As time went on and we were on the outs again with our relationship; the abuse continued on the outside of the home with name calling and the final result was being spit on at work in my face in front of a co-worker. He was later reprimanded. After attempting to end the relationship for good; my life was threaten with a gun on the table and being told to leave. As I reflected on my past relationship with my daughter's father; I began to move on with my life and began to date. The final episode of abuse resulted in being thrown down a flight of steps in front of his male friends and me filing charges with the police department; which resulted in my abuser being charged with second degree assault.

Now that I am older and no longer with my abuser for well over 16 years; I can be a beacon of light for other women who are or have been in this situation and provide words of wisdom and knowledge. Currently, I reflect on my past and where GOD has brought me from and where he continues to take me too and that is to help young women like you!

Lost Thoughts

Tearra "Truth Reality" Walker

    Being abused physically, mentally and emotionally left me with not only wounds but some that would become infected. A wound properly cared for can heal with time and do so with little to no complications. But there are some wounds that we do not allow to heal, sometimes directly or indirectly we pick, get picked and allowing picking... Infection

    Infection starts to set in and causes so many issues beneath the skin that we don't know what's happening until the damage is done and the effects are starting to spiral out of control. This spiraling can happen for the duration of your life or you can stop running and face it head on.

    I know it may sound lame or even sound like a lot; but because I've been there; I am sharing with you how important it is for you to be bold with yourself, your emotions and truths.

    There are a lot of things we can be embarrassed or ashamed about, but it's a waste of time. Accept that no one is perfect, that we all make mistakes. Accept that everyone no matter their color, social status or bank account we have all been and will continue to be hurt. What we can change is how we choose to care for the wound are you going to allow it to be infected or deal with it immediately with proper care?

    I experienced the most painful of painful moments when my mother left me; but in all honesty looking back 20 years ago. It was one of the best things that could have happened to me, and so is everything else that was designed to wound and/or infect me. I have found that in every moment that is harmful, confusing or just down right bad, that there is ALWAYS and I mean ALWAYS something good that comes from it. Now you may not find out what that good thing is but I promise (and I don't like making promises) but I promise that for EVERY Negative there is a Positive.

    Remember, you were built for GREATNESS not for Failure. You were built to LAST not to crumble under the pressures of life. So TRUST at no time in life, are you the only one who has or is going through anything. And as long as there is breath in your body and a GOD all around you, you will never be alone. Keep your head up and attack those situations head on; not later.

The Wrong Kind of Love
Brittany Williams

    I was born in New Jersey in November, 1989. My father's side of the family lived in New Jersey and Philly and my mother's side lived in the metropolitan area. They both attended college in Pennsylvania and stayed in New Jersey after graduating. Not long after they moved to Maryland closer to my mother's side of the family. My childhood was pretty fun. I loved to laugh, play outside, and sing. I went to Catholic Schools so I wasn't exposed to too much violence and negativity in my earlier years which was a blessing and curse.

    We lived in an apartment in Maryland which was so small but it was huge to me because my parents made the apartment a home. I remember funny stories like imitating my mother as she gathered the trash and threw it down the chute. I thought it looked fun so I gathered my stuffed animals; put them in a trash bag, and down they went. My mother was furious but it was so funny to me. There are so many memories I remember like that just having fun without a care in the world. We eventually ended up moving in with my grandmother. There were seven people living in that house including my younger sister. This is where my life turned and home didn't feel like home anymore. I remember always wanting to stay outside because loud screaming arguments would fill my ears as if it was normal. Don't get me wrong my family loved each other but my father's substance abuse in the mix did more harm than good. I never knew he was on drugs as a child but I recognized his actions towards people would change from happy to mad quickly but that was my dad so I accepted and still loved him regardless.

    I'm not sure how long we stayed with my grandmother but at the age of six we ended up moving to D.C. Living in that house was like living in world wind. We would be ok one day but others would have Satan's name written all over us. My mom and dad always argued about money and his where abouts. I remember one day my dad took my mom's purse trying to get money (for drugs) and ran downstairs with it. She tried to take her purse back but he wouldn't budge. I yelled and said, "Give her purse back." He yelled at me to be quiet so I shut my mouth in silence once he got in my face. Protecting my mother wasn't an option. Just like at my grandmother's house, I would never want to stay inside so I would leave the house when chaos struck.

    One day I was over my friend's house where we were chilling like girls do. In my mind I thought I was escaping the heat from my house but I actually entered the flame. We were watching TV and suddenly she had a brilliant idea of "experimenting." Her family had porn in the house and she decided we should act out the moves. Even though she wasn't much older than me she was bigger than me and I felt I had to comply. I don't want to get detailed but let's just say whatever a man has done to a woman sexually, I did to her. At a very young age I was very familiar with her body parts more then I knew of myself. At the time in my young mind I felt I had to keep it hidden just like my home life which I was a pro at doing. Growing up in secrecy made me a professional liar with a poker face to match to make my lie believable. Our sexual relationship went on from the age of 6 to about 13 or 14 years old. From the age of six I battled with that lust demon. It wasn't my choice but I had to deal with the cards I was dealt. I never told anybody because I got use to it and molestation wasn't in my vocabulary to call it that. I felt disgusting within my body and hated the site of myself. I covered my emotions with fake confidence and fought any person who thought they could get over. I had the worst temper and cared about no one but myself.

    I thought I couldn't be touched because I developed the mindset that no one would hurt me physically or emotionally anymore. I either lashed out or kept the anger in, which in addition to the molestation caused me to act out sexually as a teenager. I lost my virginity at 15 years old. The encounter with boys was different from the childhood situation because guys did all the work, I didn't have to do too much. It felt good to be wanted when I didn't feel loved in my own household. I understand now my parents didn't make me feel this way on purpose but my father's substance abuse and my mother trying the best she could to keep our family together was her focus. Her family was the same way so all she knew was anger as well. Satan had a trap set. By the age of 16, I had sex with not that many men but countless times. My body was so numb and I didn't care how I used it.

     I met a guy who I thought would be different from the others. Of course that is how females think when they don't know any better. I knew him for a long time so, I trusted him with my deepest feelings and emotions. We shared similar stories because his childhood wasn't great and he needed to be loved like I felt I did. I didn't realize two people who felt the same hurt should NOT be in a relationship. Everything was great in the beginning but isn't the honeymoon period always great? We started to get comfortable with each other enough to be intimate. The relationship didn't change when we started but sometime later something did. The love turned to lust and abuse. I don't know where it came from but it was like it just happened one day. Just like the molestation, I got use to the beatings. That was the love I felt I needed because it was something missing in my life and at the time he was there. That childhood anger turned to rage. We were totally unhealthy for each other.

     My family moved from D.C. to Maryland when I turned 16. I couldn't fully enjoy that house in the first years because my home became his. I snuck him in at night because he had nowhere to stay. In my mind, as long as he was with me I knew he was safe. We were addicted to each other and we started taking over each other's lives. We both were jealous of each other's whereabouts; we had to know what the other person was doing, like we were each other's obsession. Our minds were SCREWED UP! We had so many demons in us and we shared each other's pain so we felt it was nowhere else we could turn. I put my family through pure hell. I lost the respect of my sister and I tore my mother's heart out. She had to watch her child deteriorate right before her eyes and she couldn't do anything about it. I was blinded by the "love" I thought I needed.

    Sometimes he would stay at my house and sometimes he would find a place to stay. He didn't come "home" one night and he called me to tell me he couldn't go to the house he was staying at. He wanted me to be with him where he was. So what does a person "in love" do, run away. I packed a bag and ran out the door. My mother, grandmother, and sister were in the house and never saw it coming. I can say that was an outer body experience to actually leave my home and never look back. They chased me until they couldn't anymore. I hurt my family tremendously that day and promised I would never do that again. I ended up at the train station waiting on him to come get me. Twenty minutes went by but it seemed like an hour. He came to where I was and we went back to his residence (the streets). We slept at bus stations, train stations, crack head houses, and pretty much whoever would take us in. I was a run away with no home when I had a home but I left it all for him. Of course the abuse and anger didn't stop. The more anger he showed the more anger I built up inside. I ended up going back home after constant begging from my family. I was very stubborn, very naive and very full of myself, and I didn't care about the bigger picture or reality.

    The final straw that made me say "this is enough" was when we were in the house and Satan did not let up. We were going back and forth about nothing. He decided he wanted to leave so he got in the shower. I took a shower as well but I went to my mother's bathroom. Of course he had an attitude because he was so use to the intimate showers we would take. He saw I started changing. I made sure I finished taking a shower when he did because I didn't want him to come and try to fight me while I was defenseless and unbalanced because of the water. At this point I'm in my towel and I walk to my bathroom where he was. I went to grab my cleanser and stringent for my face but of course just walking out of the bathroom would have been too easy. He grabbed the stringent to try to take it out of my hand which caused it to splash in my eyes. For those who are not familiar with stringent, it has alcohol and many other chemicals that could cause serious damage to the eye.

    I thank God it was just a burn and not permanent damage. I run downstairs to clean my eyes and get something to drink. By this time he is fuming. He comes downstairs and starts an argument. I'm standing there rolling my eyes and waiting for his delusion to end. In my mind I knew different facial expressions would piss him off but honestly that's all I could call my own. I gave my heart, mind, and soul to him so rolling my eyes meant more than just the action. He gets really angry and throws the drink in my face. Now in addition to the stringent I now have Arizona green tea in my face. I couldn't catch a break. I wipe my face and rage filled my body to capacity. I have never been that mad and by that time I didn't care if I lived or died. It didn't matter if he lived or died. I just knew that he wasn't going to keep treating me like trash when I knew I was more than that. I walked over to the sink to get away from him. He follows me and tries to tackle me but I didn't go down because the sink was behind me. He tries to tackle me twice. By the second time I had enough because in addition to trying to tackle me he stated he was going to kill me. My mind was already at death so I said, "I WILL KILL MYSELF!" I grabbed the knife; he tried to take the knife out my hand, and the knife turned from me to him. Yes, I stabbed him.

    I ran out the house with the knife in my hand because I was so devastated that I just harmed someone. I'm not a killer or violent but at the moment my anger lashed out of my body and reacted. He was hurt really bad so I called the ambulance for him. When they came they asked him what happened. He lied and said someone else did it to protect me. They took him to the hospital and gave him bandages and pain pills to take. A couple weeks went by and I realized I couldn't do this anymore. I called him and told him I wanted to break up with him. He was furious but for some reason at that very moment I felt free. I knew he could possibly come to my house and cause havoc but for the first time I felt good.

    He didn't take the news well so he put a warrant out for my arrest. I was picked up a couple weeks after and questioned by the police. The officer then took me to the Maryland jail and booked me. Throughout that whole process the officers called me "stabber "and made up names to taunt me. It was the worst day of my life. My bond was set for 45,000 dollars and I was charged with 2nd degree assault with a deadly weapon. I was held overnight then my mother bailed me out.

 I thank God for her because she didn't have to come to my rescue like she did. I love her more than anything and I thank God for giving me her. The court date arrived and I was so nervous when this day came. I faced the judge, my ex didn't show up, and I heard the best words I've ever heard in my life "Case Dismissed." I was so full of joy I couldn't contain myself. Ever since I have been healing, understanding who I am, and telling my story to whoever needs to hear it. I understand that everyone goes through something but staying in that place and growing from it makes all the difference.

 To every girl or woman out there that has gone through something to cause you to feel broken inside, please do not stay quiet about it. Satan wants to be in control and keep you in bondage which will only keep your mind in the past. Understand that God is waiting with open arms to love you better than any boy can. Most of all learn how to love yourselves and be comfortable with your imperfections. It took me a long time and I'm still learning to just love and enjoy Brittany.

 I've learned to stop looking for love and to let God fill that spot. I've also learned that every situation I have been through took time to happen so it will take time to heal. I don't blame anyone or hate anyone for what has happened to me, but I will tell my story and help as many girls as I can.

 Always keep in mind, it doesn't matter what you have done or what has happened; all that matters is where you're going and that's up.

Smiling Through My Pain
Elizabeth Rowland

The sirens were the only thing I could hear or see. Imagine that at the age of eight! Well a few short hours earlier my mind frame was evolving around a sweet angelic person by the name of Amelia. The troubles for me started when a certain individual came into my life. After she came into my life fairness was no longer valid in my case. When I found out I was going to be living with her she had two daughters already and another on the way. First, was her daughter Kay she was not my biological sister. Yet, I treated her like she was. Second, was my biological sister Nia. When she was way younger we really did not have a relationship. The girl in which she was carrying Kia was the same situation. Despite me making the effort to get to know Kay she did not like me. A passion she had for making me feel not welcomed. My father is in the military and had to deploy and leave me with her. She goes by the name of Channal Doe. Eventually, it came time for him to leave me for nine long and excruciating months. When he was gone for only four months I was accused, but of what you may say? Well, I was accused of wetting the bed and not my bed either my sister Nia's bed. This incident was wrong I was put up against the wall by my throat until I could barely breathe and until I wet myself right there. I was given whooping's a lot during this time. I never said anything because after a while I started getting use to them it felt like I was her way too release her stress.

  The months went by and I waited on what seemed like forever for him to return. There was a night that Mrs. Channal decided to cook dinner for us. The food that she prepared was unspeakable and disgusting and her very own daughter threw it away. Mrs. Channal asked her daughter and I who threw the food away? Kay's response was, "She did it with her little ugly self I didn't mommy." Inside that made me feel horrible, hideous, and like trash on the streets. My response was, "I did not do it I promise." Despite me telling the truth I got slapped, punched in the face several times, and she threw me on the ground and cracked my head. I got up and she told me to get out of the house, and then she kicked me. I ran cross the streets to Mrs. Tameka's house and she noticed my head was bleeding extremely fast. Nothing she did helped my head and she even looked ways to stop the bleeding and nothing whatsoever helped me. Emergency services were called and I was rushed to MA Community Hospital on the base in which I was living at the time. This is where the doctors discovered that my cranial was cracked to very extensive measures and they needed to put me to sleep in order to perform the surgery. Upon doing this I fell into a coma. Waking up from the coma with no one beside you can be a very scary thing. The thoughts going through my head were rage, abandonment, sadness, and disappointment.

    Imagine waking up at eight years old out of a coma and no one is there with you. It made me feel like no one cared about me at all. My mind began to tell me I was nothing just like what I was told by certain people every day. I was taken by a social worker to my grandmother's house. I lived peacefully with her until the year of 2011. Cancer had begun to make its way into my family's lives forever. My grandmother Amelia taught me so many different things in my life while spending it with her. On the morning of September 4, 2011 our saint and my protector was called home. It seemed like my heart stopped beating and circulating blood without her in my life any more. I then went to live with my father again only this time Mrs. Channal no longer was in the picture. Jamie was now my new mother and I clicked to her as if she was my grandmother. I don't know what it was about her but; I loved her like she was my biological mother. My biological mother came around as often as she wanted to which was never. I quickly learned that Mrs. Jamie or my mom as I called her we had been through some of the same things. We related on so many levels. When I was developing into an adult my heart was heavy. Once everything occurred my mind frame changed. It made me think who all has actually been there for me. As an adolescent most of the time you worry about the new and latest toys. In my thought pattern it was about my future, goals, and simply staying alive. You may never experience what I went through. I am praying to God that you never will. If you are going through it now then my words to you are, "Keep your head up always and pray about it!" Courage, Prayer, and leaning on Gods everlasting arms are what got me through everything. One thing I wish could happen is Amelia's sweet grace walking right beside me in person. So for now she walks by me in spirit as my angel. God knew Amelia's pain and so he does everyone else on the face of the earth. The main and most important thing I learned is "To keep God number one and head of your life!" It is for the grace of God that you are able to be living another day. Your days here on this earth are not promised to you. Prayer is what I always was taught and now I tell everyone else who comes in my path to pray and give it to God. There were some days I wanted to just give up and terminate myself. It's like I heard a voice telling me to keep pushing! Life to me seemed over-rated in my young eyes. Thanks to the help of my grandmother, mom, dad, and family I have graduated this year. Also thanks to everyone else whether it may have been good or bad in my life time you all have helped me grow up. Yes, I still have days where I just look back over my past, and I also look forward to my bright future ahead of me.

    Growing up I felt like dirt underneath everyone's shoes and I felt as if I had no place in this earth that we live in. I now know that I can keep going forward and getting stronger day by day. In life we all have our ups and downs some more than others. We are all human what can we really do about it? At the end of each day we all should be thankful that we are still living and able to see days, weeks, months, and years. There are some people who do not live to see days let alone minutes. Treat everyone the way you would want to be treated. You never know what could or will happen in the future. Karma comes and goes at it pleases. In other words everyone enjoy the time that you have here on this planet. Do right by everyone that comes into your life and who may also walk out. It is going to seem hard at first yes I know. You can always kill someone with kindness greet them and keep moving forward. You have God on your side and that is really all you need. If you have access to a bible obtain it and read and study as much of it as you can. This is also something that I did a lot of while I was always on punishment. I was given a small pocket bible and I read every single day! You know so many people fall asleep reading about Gods word or any words for that matter. I cannot see how it is possible because the word of the Lord is very powerful and encouraging.

    My favorite scripture is Psalms 23. "The Lord is my shepherd I shall not want" take these words and live by them! Remember to pray for better days. God knows what He is doing. He may not be there when you want him, but He is on time.

My Struggles to Survive
Shanique Culler

All my life I thought I had this glow about myself but in reality it was just a shield. My innocence and love for life was stolen at the age of 11 due to molestation. This was done by 2 of my so called "family" members. This is when my shield came about. My hurt turned into hurting others. I would lash out in anger and aggression. I felt lonely and as if no one wanted me due to the childhood that I had previously had. I gave up on crying and trying to get answers. I started to seek God for answers.

When I met my husband I thought my prayers were answered and I was wrong. I was looking for love in all the wrong places. The first two years of our life was wonderful. I thought that this man really loved me and we were equal. Slowly but surely those tables turned. During our third year of dating we were at a family gathering. One of his family members called me pretty and I smiled and said thank you. This incident was the start of our down fall. That night, this man physically punched every window out of my vehicle and threatened to do physical harm to me. I left for 2 weeks. He apologized and promised he would get some help. I should have never believed him. He went to two counseling sessions and asked me to marry him. I agreed. I believed in my heart that he really loved me. Our first anniversary I spent it alone. He was out having an affair. Since I caught him, I was abused verbally and mentally to the point where I felt I deserved everything that this man had said to me. I forgave this man not thinking about the consequences or diseases that this man could bring to me.

After 4 years of allowing this man to do whatever he wanted because I was insecure about myself, I finally stood up to this man. I could see the rage in his eyes. I could hear the anger in his voice. This man physically assaulted me by slamming my head into a wall. The hole was more than 6 inches in diameter, blood was coming from my lip, and my stomach ached with this pain of his constant punches. These things continued for 2 more years. Constantly being beat because I didn't love myself enough to know it was wrong. I wallowed in self-pity daily. On March 15, 2008 I had had enough of the disrespect, physical, verbal and mental abuse. I stood up to this man yet again and told him, "I WANT A DIVORCE AND GET OUT OF MY HOUSE!" He then packed his things and left. I was at peace for the night. The next day I went about my business thinking I was free from the abuse. This man had another plan for me. I awoke that night to a man beating me. The smell of alcohol was so strong, I wanted to throw up. To my surprise it was my estranged husband who I was legally separated from. I had 4 bruised ribs, bruised joints that connect my temporal and jaw bones together and a broken finger.

    It was after my recovery I started seeking God the way I should have been doing in the first place. I got the courage and strength up to fight back. I had enough. This was the last time this man was going to hurt me in the manner that he did. On January 6, 2009 when I arrived home from work he was passed out drunk with another woman. This threw me in a rage. I politely woke her and asked her to leave my house if she wanted to live. I grabbed my bat out of my closet and had a fun filled time swinging that bat at and on him. I shattered his arm in 3 places and broke his leg. At that present time I felt great but the sadness, hurt, and pity and crying set back in. He signed the divorce papers gladly after that but there was still something missing. I couldn't talk to my family about these things because we were taught that you do not speak about what goes on in your home.

    Devastation, depression and suicidal thoughts began to set in but God came in right on time. I started praying more, seeking god, loving myself and praying for others. My shield slowly began to turn into my glow. I started praising God more because I knew that he would make a way out of no way. The Lord blessed my abundantly in so many ways. I rejected so many invitations to go out on dates, hang out and even games. I needed to work on myself and learn to love God more. Once I finally loved God more than myself, I was sent an angel. I declined this man the opportunity to take me out for 2 years. He was very persistent. I prayed day in and out for him to leave me alone. I was told by a stranger one day, "That man is your blessing. Stop running away from your blessing." I agreed to go to lunch and he has been right there ever since then. We have been married for 3 years now with a set of twins. I wake up thanking God for his mercy when I don't deserve it. I'm blessed that I was not killed and I can tell my story.

This poem is for you...

You are Strong

Never give up the strength that is inside you because you are strong. Strength comes from hardships struggles that you did not surrender to. You are worth the fight. Fight through the bad because God will bless you with the good abundantly and add to it. Let go what can never be fixed. Place it at God's feet because the battle is not yours. Always remember that you are smarter than and twice as beautiful as you think.

Let's Pray

Heavenly Father, I come to you in the humblest manner I know how, bowed before you offering up every soul of those abused. Father there is no other help I know. I am asking you to have mercy upon your children. LORD none of them expected abuse, some have been deceived, some taken advantage of, some wondering how they ever got to this point, some confused, some disappointed, some ashamed and most don't know how to escape. My LORD JESUS, I am asking you to stretch forth your nail scarred hands and touch them mentally, physically and spiritually and allow your healing salve to sooth away their hurt and pain. My LORD I am asking you to heal, and restore them. Those that can't forget, give them peace, those that now lack confidence, give them self-love, those that blame themselves, give them understanding and let them know it's not their fault. Those that didn't fight back, give them strength to move on, those that didn't protect their children, remove the burden, those that didn't want to leave, let them know that you provided a way of escape so they could live. My LORD some died in their abuse, some never got away, some never recovered and Father, I ask that you receive their wounded souls and give them eternal joy. LORD please have mercy on the abusers, please have mercy on the abusers, please have mercy and don't let them have to live through what they have put others through, don't let it fall on their children, please change their hearts and minds. The same hands they used to hurt make them now heal with those hands, the same arms they used with force, make them now hug with them, the same feet that once stomped upon your sons and daughters, make them now praise you with them. Change their name from abuser to Christian

In JESUS name, Amen!

~I'm Not Perfect but I'm Worth It~

But God showed his great love for us by sending Christ to die for us while we were still sinners.
Romans 5:8

She Is Worth More
Carrie Shaw

Into this world she came
Not knowing her true name
Love wasn't part of her life
Fighting, anger and strife
A roof over her head
But her spirit seemed dead
No direction or guidance given
Didn't feel this life worth living
Memories and dreams collided
Facts and truth undecided
Hurts and trust in a whirl
Hard-headed stubborn girl
Body given, no self-worth
Maybe mother shouldn't have given birth
Blames herself for everything
Unaware of what tomorrow may bring
She cries out
And lets no one in
Empty days and lonely nights
There has to be something more
She hears from heaven's door
He whispers, "I am here. I've always been.
Come to me and let me in."
The days seem brighter
Her burden lighter
Could He Be
The love she needs
Can she trust the Lord Above
Can she really receive His Love
I will protect you my child, she hears Him say
In His arms she will stay

"I AM"

NaKyiah K. Nichols

I am anointed and appointed
I wonder about where my gifts will take me
I hear the joyous sound of the angels as they watch over me
I see spirits being set free
I want to stay the humble me
I am anointed and appointed
I pretend I am a bird so I can fly away
I feel an angel wing upon me
I touch the hem of his garment
I pray I won't let go
I cry for others sorrows
I am anointed and appointed
I understand his will
I say I believe
I dream one day to be with him
I try to stay strong
I hope to one day see his face
I am anointed and appointed
I wish I was more like him
I cherish his love for me
I strive to be what he called me to be
I expect the most of him and even more from me
I realize I cannot change the past but I can redirect the future
I am that I am
I am anointed and appointed

Who Am I
Carrie Shaw

I am not just a woman.
I am a woman God created to achieve great things.
I am not just a daughter.
I am a daughter, who honors her parents.
I am not just a sister.
I am a sister, who lovingly supports her siblings.
I am not just a friend.
I am a friend, who encourages you.
I am not just a mother.
I am a mother, who teaches and builds you up.
This is who I am!

I am not who I used to be.
I was raised in a home where I never really knew if I was loved. I know I was an unwanted pregnancy. I was conceived while my mother was on birth control. To make matters worse, I was a girl. My parents told me they never wanted girls. I never felt good enough.

Life shouldn't define us.
I believe my parents did the best they could with the knowledge and abilities they thought they had. As a young child there were many times when I felt unsafe. I never believed my parents protected me as well as they should have. Several times men would try to hurt me, but I told no one. I built a wall of emotional protection. No one would get pass it.

Parents and siblings shouldn't define us.
I was a sarcastic kid, which caused me trouble with my parents. My brothers and I didn't get along well. I was beat up and abused by my older brother several times. My parents seemed to blame me and my mouth. Shame set in.

Peers shouldn't define us.
As a teenager, sex and alcohol became my friend. It allowed me to escape from family life. I wanted something to numb the pain. I

thought sex was love and I chased after it because I didn't have love from my family. Lack of worth began to develop.

Media shouldn't define us.
As an adult I allowed the magazines and television to tell me what I should look like. I exercised and dieted for years. Never did I look like the models I struggled, my whole life to feel accepted. I felt fat, ugly and undesirable. My self-esteem died.

I allowed God to show me who I am.
I know who I am and whom I am loved by. It was hard at first to understand, but I get it now. I thought love had to be tangible to feel it. I struggled to feel God's love. He loves me. He desires for me to love Him. I sense His presence. He has shown me my value, my worth and a sense of who I am. My parents may not have wanted me but God did. He has a plan for me and I will follow Him all the days of my life. He fills me with His presence. He gives me a purpose. He makes me feel beautiful. I am wonderfully and beautifully made.

My past does not define me, my parents do not define me, and the world does not define me. My God defines me.

For I Am Me

Shanique Culler

You can wear many disguises
So no one near or far can see,
Clothes, wigs and glasses mean nothing
For I am me.
The layers of your lies
The deceitfulness in your voice,
Me loving and trusting you
Was completely my choice.
The destruction I let you bring into my life
Not knowing where to start,
Crying, running and hiding
Pains began to settle in my heart.
Images of hurtful words and voices in my head
While searching, looking and trying to discover the Lord,
His grace, mercy and undying love for me
Became my shield and most powerful sword.
Rubbing, scrapping and peeling of my skin
Under God's fruitful tree,
Shows the precious gift of love
Blessed and highly favored given to thee.
Smiles that begun to show
Love that began to shine,
The reality of the pain I once felt
Started to disappear and life became kind.
No matter the struggles of life
The hurt, lies and beating from a he or she,
Just know that God's undying love comforts you

So I am seeking me, for I am me…..
Love yourself and Blessing to you

Letter to My Daughters & My Little Black Girl Self from A Grown Up Me

Fisiwe Zwana Freeman

Don't be who you want to be
Wants are transient
Be who you need to be
Needs are life-sustaining
Fight tooth and nail for authenticity
Be creative but be honest
Especially with yourself
Learn the difference between your imagination and your truth
whatever you know for sure will change but God so, don't build plans on assurances
Except for His Flow into the need to conquer what stands before you
Whatever it may be and
Become the fullness of that moment
Learn how it feels to ripple with accomplishment
Recognize how it feels to give up for fear
Be determined to choose
And value the outcome
Dare to defy the thing that takes your breath away
Take a moment to pray Inhale anyway then breathe life into your dreams
And reinvent yourself over and over again
Don't regret time in the valleys between your mountains
Reflect, rest and be renewed
For your next climb will be your greatest yet
"My little black girl self is timeless
She is my past she's with me now"

Pretty Little Thick Girl!

NaKyiah K. Nichols

For I am a pretty girl as far as I know
For I am a thick girl as far as I see
For I am a pretty little black girl as far as I've heard
People bash and criticize me but I don't take it personally
Because I love who I am and I love who I become.
The strong, beautiful, little thick black girl I see in me
And not what they see in me, for I have been lied on and talked about
But once again I don't let it get to me, because I see the leader in me
A strong, beautiful, smart young lady is what I seem to be
For I feel confident in myself and because I learn from my mistakes
I know right from wrong so I re-direct my path and all my wrong
So now they can't get to me because I don't take it personally
For I am a pretty girl, as far as I know
For I am a thick girl, as far as I see
For I am a pretty little black girl and a strong, beautiful young lady to be

Who I'm Created to Be

Carolyn Terry

Who do you say that I am
I am, that I am, that I am
Not what you say that I am
I am everything that God created me to be.
Years of never knowing my true identity
Wanting you to love every part of me
Has led me down a path of uncertainty
I am everything that God created me to be.
Desperately I believed every word you spoke to me
Even in your late nights of having fun and cheating
And me with my morning, noon and night beatings
I am everything that God created me to be.
Learning that my self-esteem was at level zero
And the confidence I didn't know that was in me
As I sit and I wait and I wait on my super hero
I am everything God created me to be.
Finally tired of the control I freely give
I know in my heart He's given me the key
The spirit is telling me it's time to live
I am everything God created me to be.
You've stolen years and years of my life
And now I know exactly who I need
I'm a daughter, mother, grandmother and wife
I am everything God created me to be.
No I'm not perfect, but yes I'm worth it
You didn't get to choose my destiny
God reached way down and rescued me
I am everything God created me to be.
With bow down head and knees to the floor
Thanking and praising him for loving more
And now I'm free and loving me
And yes, I am exactly who God created me to be.

You Are a Queen
Raiya Coates

Females today say that they love the skin that they are in
But I bet you a million dollars that they are continuously crying within
Wondering always is it me
But do they not understand that its society
You are stunning,
But if you need a reminder then look in the mirror
And if that don't work
Than ask me
Because I would never knock you down and burry your feelings under your feet
It's okay to love yourself
It's okay to be who you are
It's okay to know that your greatness
But there is always a women who says that you're worthless
But hey you can't change them all
Let change start with you
Because you are a beauty
Always study your ABC'S
Always be classy
Because the next ratchet thing that comes along isn't worrying about making you happy
That cute dude that just wanna bone
He not worthy to even stand near your thrown,
Your royalty
And love yourself
Because perfection can't be perfected
So COMPREHEND WHEN I SAY...
You Are a Queen

Spirit

NaKyiah K. Nichols

Dear Spirit,

I'm writing you in regards to my feelings. I believe that you take advantage of me and my kindness. I've allowed you to treat me this way long enough. You attempt to bully me mentally with negative thoughts desiring them to form into actions and I don't appreciate it. You can no longer blackmail me with mistakes from my past telling me that I'm not going to make it and that the troubles and disappointments will last. While growing up in church I would hear a wise person say, "Devil you lose!" Spirit, today you lose! I am not going to have you pushing me around as if I'm somebody on the street; I won't let you treat me any kind of way as if I have no knowledge of the courage, strength or power I have within. I am beautiful this I know although there are times you try to convince me otherwise. You can no longer put me down, talk about my weight or the concern of my brown eyes, because I am a child of God and I beautifully created in his image. I would like to say thank you for helping me realize who I truly am. Thank you for helping me finds my inner self where the beauty really lies. I am a strong young lady even if you don't see it in your eyes. You can no longer hurt me through your words or actions because now it's you and not me that I despise. Besides, my Father reminded me that if he be for me it's more than you and the whole world that is against me. Today is this day that I declare to no longer fear you or feel any form of shame but thank you because if it wasn't for you I would be to blame.

Yours truly the Blessed and Favored,

NaKyiah K. Nichols

True Love Awaits

Lakita Stewart-Thompson

I am beautiful made in the image of He
I am a fresh breath of dust
I am made fearfully and wonderfully
I am marked and made clean
I am whiter than the purest snow where the sky is clear and the clouds so eloquently flow
I am foreknown before the foundations of the world with a life to share
I am uniquely and constructively built, like a garden of soft white lilies on a blooming valley field
I am made without a spot or blemish, my love sealed our commitment with His lucid yet charming words
IT IS FINISHED
I am numbered, each hair on my head
I am preserved, purposed, sound, and spiritually led
I am covered, kept, whole, and free; I am the savoring essence of all impurities
Where true loves waits without regrets or mistakes
I am blood stained yet uncontaminated
I am Mary, Mary is me, Untouched, Untainted, But impregnated with endless possibilities
I am a dream come true; I am a pioneer of purity; I am change; I am the He that lives on the inside of me
I am Pure, Pure is me; I am living in pursuit of my planned Destiny; I am called by name, yes Mrs. Pure
I am confident, confident is me; I am secure
I vow to cherish Him; Till death do us part
Pure is not only the love of my life
He is on the inside of my heart
On this day, I thee wed to my Mr. Pure
I am Pure, Pure is me
Where I love He and He surely loves and appreciates me
The only true love that waited for my virginity

A love worth all of me
Where true love waits, without regrets or mistakes
I am Pure, Pure is me
A place where every woman wants or should be
Wanting to trade places with me, I am a woman of Destiny
Who is pure, who is clean
I am preserving Pure, He is my sacred virginity
I remember there is a she
A sister, a friend, a lost girl
Who is closely yet intimately watching me
As I
I Am
A Woman of Virginity
A Virtuous and Phenomenal Woman
Yes, That's Me, that's you
Where true loves waits without regrets or mistakes

I am Destinee, Destiny is me

Destinee M. Thompson

PURPOSE
It was God's plan to create me
I am Destinee, destiny is me
I was destined, yes purposed to be

Before I was formed in my mother's womb
God knew me
He made me fearfully and wonderfully
Set Apart Purposely
This aborted every plan tried by the enemy

PURPOSE
It was God's plan to create me
I am Destinee, destiny is me
I was destined, yes purposed to be

For God created my inmost being
He knit me together and numbered every hair on my head
This binds every lie that the enemy has ever said:
Destinee you are not growing in your mother's womb
Your mommy was on bed rest at 5 months, you are going to be
a handful
You will be on Ritalin before the age of two
You are too bad; I want nothing to do with you
I often heard them say I was off the chain too
You will never amount to anything is what they said at school
Your daddy doesn't even want you, is what I heard grown-ups
say
I even said I wanted to kill myself one day
You're just a spoiled brat
With your inability to focus, cannot be that smart
We assume its ADHD or parental care you lack
You're not normal, something must be wrong with you

You always want to be the center of attention
And you're not so beautiful

PURPOSE
It was God's plan to create me
I am Destinee, destiny is me
I was destined, yes purposed to be

Purpose is the reason for which something exist
This is why my mother was unsuccessful at her suicidal attempts
Since destiny is purposed and plan to be
It exposed every plan disguised by the enemy
I survived
Abandonment, rejection, and near death tragedies
Even being abused verbally, mentally, and physically
At the hands of those who claim to love me and even those who are supposed to educate us
After being touched inappropriately, I developed this strong spirit of perversion and lust
Battling great spirits that has tried to take residence inside
Resisting the spirit of suicide that tried to hunt me at the age of 5
But by the grace of God and many prayers
I am still alive

PURPOSE
It was God's plan to create me
I am Destinee, destiny is me
I was destined, yes purposed to be

I come from family where generational curses on both sides are disguised
Where nobody wants to talk and work out the issues in their lives
Bondage that's rooted so deep, it unbearable to the human eye
No wonder I had uncontrollable tantrums
Where all I would do is cry
Never understood the magnitude of the curse anger and rage
That was illegally adopted on my insides

But I am realizing my purpose is necessary and I bind every
single lie

P U R P O S E
It was God's plan to create me
I am Destinee, destiny is me
I was destined, yes purposed to be

Mommy showed me in God's word that I am overcome by the
word of my testimony
My purposed was inevitable
His plan will be fulfilled
Though in my short years here
By His stripes I am healed
Healed from the past and many pains to come
At only 7 years old
I know where my joy and strength come from

P U R P O S E
It was God's plan to create me
I am Destinee, destiny is me
I was destined, yes purposed to be

Let's Pray

Our Father who art in Heaven, I come to you with thanksgiving in my heart. Asking you to have mercy upon me, LORD, I need you, LORD, I need you, Yes, LORD, I need you. Please forgive me for I have fallen short. I know you rose for me and you know all about me but I still feel unworthy. I can't be who they want me to be. I can't change who I am, I can't. One touch, just one touch is all I need from you my Lord JESUS. Receive me, I want to serve you, change me so that I can help others with my mistakes. Help me to guide other with my journey, help me to lead the blind with my sight, help me to heal others with my scars....in JESUS name, AMEN!

~Learning to Live Without You~

God blesses those who mourn, for they will be comforted. Romans 5:8 (NLT)

The LORD is close to the brokenhearted; he rescues those whose spirits are crushed.
Psalm 34:18 (NLT)

It Didn't Break me, Only Made me Stronger: Life after Death

Carolyn Terry

  Nothing could have prepared me for this part of my life in a million years. To be young and experience the losses I have already at the age of 54, my father, brother, children, and my mother. Lord I wasn't prepared for this, but then again you did prepare me for a few of them. You hear many stories of how someone is left feeling at the loss of a love one, but never really understand it until it hits home. As a mother you always thought that your children will be burying you, but not in today's society death has no age. My dad died of cancer, my baby brother died of throat cancer, and to have witness this in his final days was unreal for me, for many reasons. Even though we grew up together in our younger days we drifted apart down through the years, but we were in contact occasionally. I thank God that he allowed my brother and me to reconnect, ask for forgiveness and be there in his final days.

  Even in his sickness my brother let me know that he was alright and that he loved me. The most devastating deaths that I believe has knocked the wind out of me were my children and the death of my mom. I remember as if it was yesterday, my daughter Jewel 25 years of age diagnose with ovarian cancer. I remember standing in the hospital and the doctor telling me that she has cancer in three areas of her body, my mind in disbelief while my body went numb standing there as though I had just stop breathing myself. In my mind isn't this a disease that only old people get? I guess not because the evidence is right before you, illness has no age limit. No one here with me, I picked up the phone and called her grandmother telling her the news that not only paralyze me but the entire family.

  How could this happen to such a beautiful young woman that knew the meaning of family. The one person that was the glue to the family from birthday celebrations, family reunions, cookouts whatever gathering was going on, you could always expect Jewel to be present. As days, weeks, months and the year went by my faith in God was what was keeping me standing. I remember the many conversation God and I had about strengthen me on this journey. Then the time came that moment you walk in the house and you hear the spirit say it's time for you to let her go and you freeze. Who wants to let go of their love ones, but then again who wants them to suffer? As a mother you do what is best for your child and you make the ultimate sacrifice, release and let go. The blessing was that because of the time God allowed me to take care of her, bring her home and let her spend her final days with people that loved her, the transition was not as easy I thought it would be. She looked up at me, our eyes connected and then I knew this was our goodbye. As I held her hand she began to close her eyes with the beauty of an angel that she was. I learn that expected deaths aren't as bad as the unexpected deaths, which leads me to me to my next death, my son. Talking about the unexpected, a typical day, you go to work and this particular day you have a doctor's appointment and you wait for the husband to come pick you up and realize he's running late so you call him. He answers, the voice on the other ends doesn't sound as normal and you hear the words man (James) is gone. Well because I was so use to him staying in trouble with the law my first instinct is what has he done now? Silence comes across the phone and the one thing no mother wants to hear, Man is dead. Unable to move, this can't be happening it's only been 2 and half years since I've buried my first child, God there is no way you are doing this to me again, why Lord, why? Rushing to the crime scene and seeing all this yellow tape does not mean my son is dead, I have not seen the body. The detective did not let me in because hubby had already identified the body and all I remember him saying is you don't want to see him like that. My question to him, are you crazy that's my baby in there, he needs his mother, but he's gone. They have just now brought out his body after 5 hours covered up and I'm still not convinced that's my son. Watching the news back and forth about this shooting in PG county on

Swann Road, still not convince that's my son. Here we are a week later time to view the body and there he is, laying there as if he's asleep, handsome as ever, still not convince he's dead.

Now the day of the funeral, the church is packed and somewhere in me I knew that his killer was there. I stand at his casket watching the faces of the viewers that comes by to see if I can feel or see anything that may help catch my son's killer, and there it is that one person that comes by looks down and smirks. As I'm watching him he looks up and sees me looking at him and changes his expression. Now it time for the service to start and I as a mother have to give my final thoughts. As I stand there and look around the church of all the young people that were there, the words that came out was vengeance is my mine said the Lord, I don't want anyone retaliating my son's death, no mother needs to stand where I'm standing for the second time burying her child (children), and if you are in here I have to forgive you for taking my sons life. Now we all know this has to be God because the flesh would have taken a different route, but when you live a life for Christ the best you know how, He will not allow you to dwell in anything that is not pleasing in His sight. What it did do to me was, I began to start playing detective on my own, I found myself on the streets asking questions, dropping hints, showing up at the police station probably more than they wanted to see me and spending numerous days at my sons gravesite. Finally I realize that I was allowing myself to grieve more than I needed to and I wasn't letting my son rest in peace. I couldn't help it, being a mom is all I know in life and death, I wanted answers and as a mother I felt like I was letting him down. Sad thing he was changing his life around and the streets wasn't going to let that happen. God did allow me to see just how many lives my son touched on that day from the youngest to the oldest and even after the funeral was over.

    I was amazed at the many of people that came in the church with a picture of him on their shirt and they were all different. Every person had their own memories of my son in their own way. After 11 years of my daughter's death and 8 years for my son's death I can finally say that the grief process is over, at least for them. When I look back the blessing for me was that God chose me for their mother, not because of anything special but because He knew He could trust me with the assignment that would come later in their lives. God knew that even in a short time that these two children would bring me the joy that I had been searching for all my life, a family of my own. Thinking this is it for me, I am now hit with another death, one that I had no idea would leave me feeling so empty because of the history, but it doesn't matter about the past it has everything to do with the right now, the future. This brings me to my mom's death, Lord you got to be kidding me, you have put me in the same position you had me in 11 years ago. How much do you think I can endure?

    Three years ago my mom came to live with me and my husband and only God knew what was about to take place, because this was a woman of strength that has never been seriously sick in 86 years of her life.

    In 2014 Mama was given this big birthday party with all her family and friends, the look on her face was priceless, never to know it was her last birthday with us. I remember my mom saying if I never have another birthday I will always remember this one my 87th birthday. The unexpected happens in 2015 mom is diagnose with colon cancer, Lord really, I don't believe this. Here again standing alone at the hospital and hearing these words have taking me back to a place that I once was familiar with. Unbelievable, why me Lord, my heart has just speeded up its beat and numbness once again has attacked my body. Here is a woman that had eight children, was unable to keep us and yes there were my angry moments, but years ago I forgave my mom and my relationship with her right now was what was important, the bonding we had only to realize that it was soon coming to an end. My mom made it clear, no chemo I just want to enjoy my life while I can. That day they told her, I remember mommy crying and saying that she didn't want to leave her babies, my thought was mommy this time you don't have a choice. The doctor told me she only had months and at this point I want to make everything happen that she hasn't done yet.

    One day in the bathroom I remember asking God for one more Mother's Day and I heard it just as clear as if He was in the bathroom with me, He said, "I'll give you Easter." Mom became disabled to do for herself and I knew this killed her because she was so independent, but now she was stricken to her bed. I began to journal about my mom sickness every day until it got close and I could no longer pick up the pen about three days before her death. I bath her, fed her when she would eat which wasn't often; made sure she took her pain medicine and even moved across the room from her just to be close to her in the midnight hours. Imagine waking up in the mornings and standing in the doorway just to make sure she was breathing every morning, and each day she was I would look up and say Lord thank you for one more day. Because I had been in this place before I knew that death was just around the corner. Even in her sickness she was grateful for the care we were giving her, always saying thank you.

Whenever I would walk in the room her eyes would light up with the joy of seeing me and she would say there goes my baby and just smile. Most difficult conversation was when she looked at me and asked me was she going to die? I had to be honest with her, Ma yes one day you will, but right now let's just live and enjoy. You could have brought me for free when she asked me this question; I had to leave out after I answered her so that she wouldn't see my tears. The woman that never took care of me I was now responsible for taking care of her. God will take a painful situation and turn it into a joyous one.

Yes, I got joy out of taking care of my mom it was a blessing because it brought us just that much closer. Getting off from work I looked at my phone to make sure that it was turned up so I could hear it when it rang only to see I had a miss call from my husband, and then I knew she was gone. Ma must have had her last talk with God and told Him she was ready and decided it was time to leave me. I always knew that she would do it when I wasn't home, and she did on April 10, 2015 between 1:00 and 1:30 am in the morning while on my way in from work. When I got home there she was lying in the same position she was in from that morning as if she knew, I'm just positioning myself for the transition. She had such a peaceful look, my mommy, my best friend and my shero.

Looking back on my journey of death I know that it was God that kept me in my right mind. I know that it was all for a purpose rather this book or to help others along the way that might experience this in their life time. The blessing is because I was obedient to His will and His way my grieving moments for my mom wasn't long at all. I made it through Mother's day, probably because we celebrated Mother's Day before my mom closed her eyes.

So ask me how I learn to live without them, you never do, you just take it one day at a time, don't hold on to the pain, allow yourself to breath, think about all the beautiful memories you shared and pass that love on to someone else, but most important my favorite two words, BUT GOD!

Losing my Mother
Elisabeth Budd-Brown

    Many events have shaped my life in my 30 years on this earth. There have been storms, celebrations, revelations, and breakthroughs. These have shaped the woman I am today. One of the most influential, and hardest, moments of my life occurred on September 16, 2004. It was the day I lost my mother at only 20 years old.

    I remember arguing on the phone with my boyfriend early that morning, in my dorm room. I remember hearing the phone beep and not wanting to click over because the argument was so heated--I felt as though I had to prove my point. But then a realization came over me, the only person who would be calling me that early would be my mom. So I resignedly clicked over. She had called to tell me to make sure I called my sister in Puerto Rico because there was a hurricane coming and we needed to make sure she would be alright. I remember her voice sounding so faint on the phone. She asked me if I was ok-- she could probably hear the frustration in my voice. I reassured her and attempted to rush her off the phone. She said she loved me, I said it back and we hung up.

    I can't tell you whether or not I ever finished that conversation with my ex-boyfriend. I can't tell you what else I did that day: what I ate, who I talked to, where I went, or what I wore. The only other thing I remember was the other phone call I received later that evening. My 16 year old brother called to tell me he was worried, that my father had rushed my mother to the hospital because she was having really bad headaches. She even called out of work that day, the first time in over 30 years of teaching. Something in his voice made my stomach drop. I tried to reassure him that she would be fine and that he could call me whenever he needed to, no matter the hour.

    And he did call me back later that night. He called to tell me that our mother had died. It was sudden and unexpected.

She died of a brain aneurysm. I later found out that when they got to the hospital, my mother apologized to my father for not cooking dinner that night and then collapsed. I remember being in disbelief. How could she not be there? She had always been there for everything. She was always there talking, laughing, smiling, encouraging, and taking pictures. I think she believed that her children's needs were more important than her own. She always told us that God had given her four of his best angels and that it was her job to take care of them and raise them properly.

I think the hardest thing about losing her wasn't that year, but every year since. She wasn't there for my wedding, my first child, my new jobs, or my first house. I never received another hug, kiss, or encouraging word. I have gone through it on my own, feeling like a motherless child. I often wonder at how I have fought through the pain and confusion and not become bitter. Holidays are always painful. I often look into my daughter's face and marvel. She has my mother's eyes.

My mother was a care giver. She believed in sending people little reminders that she cared. She gave advice, encouragement, and wisdom through these small packets of sunshine. I have a small album of cards she sent me from 2002-2003 that I refer to when I miss her, the most and need her advice.

Although it has been 10 years, sometimes it still feels like yesterday. I get through it through my faith and lots of prayer. I remember the values my mother instilled in me, and pass them on to my children. These values have allowed me to hear her voice and tap into her wisdom, even though she is no longer on this earth. I strive to do what is right, instead of what is easy and follow my heart. I treat others, as best I can, as I would want to be treated. And I remember to face the light, instead of the shadows. One of the biggest lessons I have taken from my mother's life was her walk with Christ. The older I get, the better I understand her constant reminders to go into your prayer closet before making any decisions. Even though my mother isn't with me physically, she lives on in my heart.

My Heart in Human Form
NaKyiah K. Nichols

From the time I was a baby until August 15, 2014 I always had one lady I could count on, my Auntie Lena. She was a true blessing to me and my mother. She was an angel sent down from heaven in human form to protect and to take care of me. My Auntie was special and she always made a way no matter what the situations were. My Auntie Lena and I had a very close relationship. I was always over her house and I was always with her. Not only was I close to her, but I was also really close to her family. I loved my auntie to death. I loved her presence and just being around her. She always had an encouraging word to give in every situation. She would always say, "The devil is a liar!" My Auntie was my angel. She never gave up on me no matter if I was in trouble or did something wrong; she would still love up on me. I talked to her at least 4-5 times a week if I wasn't over her house. Aside from my mother she was my rock, my provider, and my angel. She always lifted people spirits even when her spirit was down. Now don't get me wrong my Auntie wasn't perfect but she was the best she could be.

About a month before she died my Auntie was very sick. She was weak and unable to do for herself. I knew that it was almost that time… I spent the month of July with my auntie along with my two cousins. We had to wash her, cook and feed her too. Her two daughters and son would be there to help whenever they weren't working. One day while me and my Auntie was eating lunch and watching T.V. she broke down and started crying. She kept saying over and over how she was tired and she was ready to go. I started to cry. The feeling of someone you love being hurt and in pain is very overwhelming. We begin to talk and have a heart to heart moment. I remember her saying, "Don't ever let anyone tell you that you can't do something. You are smart and keep a close relationship with Christ." If anyone knew my Auntie they knew that she loved the Lord; until she got really sick and couldn't see (she started going blind in one eye) she would read 10 chapters from the bible every day. Even though her health prevented her from making it to church on a regular basis like she was used to, she knew God and his word for herself.

     My Auntie Lena was a woman of honor, respect, and loyalty. She was and is irreplaceable. I will always remember her and the example that she set for me. I know in my heart that she would be very proud of me and the young lady that I am. I love her and she will forever be in my heart. Mrs. Selena Bradley you were my God-mommy, my auntie, my love, my heart in human form but now you are my heavenly ANGEL.

Losing My Heart, My Best Friend, My Mother

Raven Cassidone

For I know the plans I have for you, declares the Lord, plans to prosper you and not to harm you, plans to give you hope and a future. Jeremiah 29:11

My name is Raven Cassidone I'm 24 years old, I have a blood disease called Sickle Cell Anemia; I was diagnosed with Sickle Cell at birth. My mother Lisa Cassidone also has Sickle Cell Anemia and suffered from it all throughout her life. Sickle Cell Disease is a hereditary blood disorder that affects the red blood cells and nearly over 100,000 people in the United States alone today. I along with many others suffer from Sickle Cell Disease and live with it their entire life, because currently there is no cure for this. With treatments and continuous care for Sickle Cell most patients can live a "normal life."

Unfortunately, due to the damage and several complications the disease bring, sometimes patients lose the lifelong fight with Sickle Cell Disease. On June 9th of 2007, my beautiful mother at the age of 40 years young passed away due to double pneumonia and the complications of Sickle Cell Anemia. I remember how I felt when it was time to start planning to celebrate my 16th birthday. Life was good; I was excited and ready to enjoy my "sweet 16" just like so many other young girls around that age. My best friend Mel and I both are the youngest of our families and both of our birthdays are a week apart, so it was only natural for us to do it big together. A weekend filled with fun, music, food, friends, family and a sweet sixteen bash that we would always remember. Never could I imagine that August 25, 2006 would be my very last birthday spent with my heart, my rock, my mother Lisa Cassidone.

Living with Sickle Cell was never hard when you were around; you made the fight seem easy. Never did you complain or show anything but smiles and life full of joy, you showed me the true meaning of being strong and taught me how to be a fighter. I practice this each day to reach for the things I want in life, and to never let people say I can't because of sickness.

On days like this is when I miss you the most, nights spending taking trips to the emergency room for a treatment alone. When you were alive I was never was or felt alone. You stood by my side and held my hand. This daily struggle with sickle cell was made easier when I had my soldier, my rider by my side. No matter how bad my body felt, or discouraged I was, you gave me that comfort of knowing I could fight yet another day. It hurts me so bad that you had to leave, I wasn't ready you were my best friend in pain physically and emotionally. I wish you were here to rock me and let me know everything was alright. You did that the best so strong and supportive for everybody not just me.

In 07' I was only 16 years old now at age 24 it's just some grown woman issues were I need my rock, my mother. When everyone walked out or bailed on me you were always in my corner. As my number one fan supporting me at cheerleading competitions, softball games, dance practice, model auditions, and anything I wanted to try. It didn't matter to you when everyone else said I couldn't do it you always believed I could. You use to say don't ever let sickle cell or anything or one keep you down or stop you from doing what you want. Even now today I keep that in my heart, for the things I want to do or achieve I remember you saying "Hey you're Lisa's girl you don't let these people tell you, you can't because of your sickness or anything else. If you want it then get it, and if it doesn't work at least you tried." Hearing your voice saying that in my head is what keeps me pushing to the next level, of course with the help of God. My heart sometimes smiles when I think of how much you impacted lives and how much you inspired mines in just 16 years. I thank God for the sweet time I had with you. Yes I miss you every day, a lot but I can smile knowing that I had you and as my mom you poured so much into me that has made me grow over the years. Even with eyes filled with tears I can praise God because you died saved, trusting and believing in Jesus Christ, so there is Joy knowing I will see and be with you again in paradise.

    I can't speak for anyone else but as of now in my life, it feels like losing you will always be a constant healing for me. I ask and I wonder, how do I go through mothers' day and other holidays without feeling sad or down? How do I get to a place where I'm not jealous of other daughters with their moms in the store shopping? When I feel these things people probably think, oh just get over it, but I sit and wonder, God will I ever really be over losing my mom, my best friend?

    I asked a question that for a long time stayed in my mind. Would I ever get over losing my mother? I use to think that the pain was too great, that I missed her too much. But I'm so glad, grateful that here today after 8 years of holding onto the painful journey of the grieving process, that I can say now I can smile and enjoy the memories of my mom without feeling sad or depressed. Now when I say this doesn't get me mistaken, if you ever or already gone through a major lost; it is going to be a very hard process. Losing someone like a parent, guardian, spouse, a child or sibling are the toughest to recover from. Along with myself and almost everyone across the world know that "Momma" is one of the most important to you. She is the one who loves you no matter what, she is the one who supports and keeps the family together, Momma disciplines you when you are wrong but still loves you to show you how to do right. Mom is the strong Queen who does what she has to for her babies even when if, or if dad doesn't. She's not ashamed to get on her knees to pray and cry out to God for her strength. She takes care of home and even when stressed embraces you with love and a smile while asking, "How was School?" I can go on and on about all the wonderful things that "Momma" is and I hope in some way you can relate. All of these things just give an example of how much a Mother is to a person, and the impact it can have on your life by her passing away. Now I understand the thought of that happening or like in my case has already happened is a bad experience but I having good news!

You don't have to stay in a prolonged place of sadness, depression or negative feelings. With God on your side it is okay to go through the stages of grief (Denial, Isolation Anger, Bargaining, Depression, and Acceptance) which for me took quite some time. But it can happen, my prayer is that when you come across sickness or death that you see the positive and to keep in mind the good memories you have with your loved one.

Truly His Mooky-Mook

NaKyiah K. Nichols

    My Papa played a major part of the young lady I am today. My Papa was wise and always had a sweet spirit towards to me. No matter what situation he was in he always told me that I was special and I was always going to be something in life. I truly believe my Papa from the bottom of my heart. He had a good heart, he was a good man, and was a father figure to me. My Papa would take the time out and read to me during my infant, toddler, and younger years. He always told me that I must read and learn my history so I could be smart and intelligent. If his scheduled allowed he would take time out to come to my school events to show love and support. I was his Mooky-Mook and I didn't ever do any wrong in his eyes. During the times I would feel discourage just being around him talking, laughing or just reading would uplift my spirits because of his sweet spirit. My Papa would do things that would make me laugh uncontrollably like for example, instead of saying the words in the correct order he would say them backwards. Instead of asking me do I want him to cook me some fish sticks he would say, "Mooky-Mook do you want some sticks fish?"

    One day my mom finally decided to tell me that my Papa was diagnosed with cancer and that one day will come when he will pass away. Although I believed my mother it didn't seem like my Papa was ill because all the things he could do. I never imagine life without my Papa. I couldn't I ever move on with life knowing he would never see the great things he so often spoke into my life. However, as time went on and years begin to pass I wanted to spend more time with my Papa because I noticed he begin to become physically weaker, smaller in weight, eating less and couldn't stay up to enjoy family time like he use too. I would find myself doing the things for my Papa like he did when I was younger. I would spend weekends over his house and lie next to him on the bed and read him the newspaper and some of history books that he had such a great love for.

On February 9, 2014 we received the very early morning telephone call that my Papa passed away at the Veteran's Hospital in Washington, DC. My heart stopped! I was breath taken and all I could do was cry. He was my Papa and he wasn't supposed to leave me. He was the man I could count on to be my father figure. Now what was I supposed to do without him? But God! While my family made the funeral arrangements I was informed that my Papa wanted me to minster in mime dance for his service. Since the day I found out about my Papa passing I didn't want to go to school, mime dance, or anything else. I only desired to do nothing but reflect on the memories we created and shared with one another. I felt that a part of my heart had left and was never coming back. I often would reflect on the times he gave me 101 life lessons and how he would write me poems. The day finally came when I was going to see my Papa for the very last time here on earth. I was so full of sorrow and didn't know how I was going to minister under all the pressure I was feeling. But God and only God gave me the strength, held my tears back and allowed me to stand in front of my Papa casket and minister in dance one last time for my Papa. The church was so overwhelmed from the dance that it filled the atmosphere with the presence of God with such a joyous spirit within the people that came to pay their final respects. I now find myself from time to time grabbing the telephone to call or text him to let him know the good grades I made or the positive things I accomplished in school as I often did in the past. I then realize that he is no longer here to respond but has transition to be with the Lord.

Now, I have come to a realization that there is a time and place for everyone to die rather we like it or not. So I have come to except my Papa being physically gone but forever being with me in my heart and spirit. I hold on to the thoughts and belief in my heart that I will see him again in my heavenly home. I often think of his last words to me, "God is love and love is God. You can't have one without the other Mooky-Mook. You are different and you are going to be something in life because you are smart. Stay close to the Creator." I will forever love, and cherish my hero and inspiration my Papa. I am truly his Mooky-Mook and he will always be my Papa.

Strength From The Side of the Bed
Lolita Cleveland

It was a quiet late night when I was eight years old girl when I realized that my mother was never coming back. There was emptiness and a void. I was a loved little girl who had family that showered me with love, gifts, kisses and hugs but nothing could help the feelings that I had in my heart. I ached to be loved, cared for and wanted. I felt abandoned in a world that loved me. I wanted to figure out why I was feeling sad, unloved and unwanted. As I sat on the side of my bed I began to speak out loud. My grandmother that raised me after the death of my mother at age seven had always told me that I was loved and that God was always with me and that he would never leave or forsake me.

Well this night on the side of the bed I took my grandmothers words and said out of my mouth "Lord my grandmother say you are real and that you will never leave or forsake me, if you are real I need you NOW! My mom is gone and I know my family loves me, but I feel like I am missing a part of me now that she is gone. Who will be my mother, who will show me the way, who will rub me when I am sick, who will protect me. If you are real please show me".

After sitting and talking out loud there was no one in the room so I wondered why I felt like someone was with me. I looked around and didn't see any one and then I felt an arm around me and I couldn't figure out why. I said aloud, "Lord is that you because you are the only person that I have been talking to." I felt a peace in the room and I instantly felt better, but I didn't understand why. As I set there quietly I heard a voice say, "I am with you always." I began to cry and felt better. As I went on with my eight year old life I began to meet new friends started a new school and met my best friend Rena. Rena was cool and I always spoke to her at my new school. We began to talk, phone each other and even had sleep over's. I knew Rena whole family and was treated as family by Rena parents.

      As time went on I grew into my pre-teen and teen years, those years became difficult with time do to the death of my grandmother. Again I felt lost, alone and this time angry. I moved in with my sister Marie that provided a great home and stability. However, there was this feeling of a void. I continued on with my life journey and at fourteen I made a big step to accept Jesus Christ as my personal Savior. Due to still being young I did not fully know what that meant, but I knew I felt different. As I enjoyed my teen years and learned how to drive and enjoy my friends and outings, a male family friend began to molest me. He would buy me things I liked and wanted and all I had to do was have sex with him and keep it quiet. I wanted all of the nice things, he took me wherever I wanted to go with friends and his assistance helped my sister out with raising me so I did it for over a year or so until I was sixteen. At sixteen I told him NO! He took me to the store to obtain Christmas items and when we returned back I went upstairs to get a pen and he proceeded upstairs and backed me into a corner, flung me on the bed, I cried, screamed and said NO!; but nobody could hear me. He injected me with a liquid in order to try and drug me. I told him,"TODAY it will STOP!" Before he could finish the injection, my dog bit him (I am a strong believer pet's know when there is trouble).

      After counseling and staying away from boys in fear of being raped again I stayed to myself and only surrounded myself with family and friends. As adulthood approached there was this void again. Prom, graduation and college were approaching and the pressure of this void was there. I was still angry and upset about my life and why was there so much up and down since childhood. The feeling of abandonment was there. I decided if I went to college things would get better. So I went away to college and had a great time partying, experiencing marijuana and alcohol use. I did not date much but I later meet a guy that I dated for a few years until he hurt me, by getting another girl pregnant and blaming me. The first semester grades came and I was told that I would be kicked out of college I did not know what to do. The dean said, "You are just like the rest and you will never regain focus." The feeling of abandonment came again. I did what I knew to do, this time I fell to my knees at the side of my bed and I said, "Lord you said you would never leave or forsake me" I instantly felt the arm I felt at eight years old and I realized that it was the Lord holding me in his arms. I told the Lord all about what I had been through in my life (as if he didn't know) and where I was at that moment. I said, "Lord if you show me what to do I will do it." My sister called me and told me she was proud of me fifteen minutes after I prayed. I got up and wrote out a plan. I continued on for the semester and made the dean's list, graduated college, obtained a job and I now have a master's degree, a business and an author.

    Know that God will meet you at every step in your journey you must trust and believe that he will do it. No matter what you feeling you must now that God is ALWAYS with you and he will never leave you, mistreat you, abandon you or forsake you. He will forgive you if you ask and will lead you on the path of being courageous. Be strong and courageous. Do not be afraid or terrified because of them, for the LORD your God goes with you; he will never leave you nor forsake you." Deuteronomy 31:6

My Enemy My Angel...
Minister Tanya L. Baylor

From the time we connected I despised you and you despised me too. We knew one another as just enemies. The moments we could speak positively about each another, we preferred to defame each other's character with words of negativity and profanity. While in one another's presence at church or family functions the eyes would roll, the sneaky laughter would become loud and small altercations would arouse us. Nothing happened for us to feel the way we did we were just was two stubborn, hard headed, know it all's that didn't think twice about being friends. Until that day came, the day my blessing NaKyiah, and your Nuk was born, our bond became true. She mended the anger, bitterness and brokenness we both carried for one another because God knew the journey we had to travel I needed someone dear who would eventually treat me like a daughter and I like a mother. Life for us went beyond the marriage that connected us.

I knew I wanted to be the best mother I could be and the life I was living could no longer be for me. As I became a single parent and the struggles were my reality, deep down in your heart I knew you desired to help me heal. I always kept my blessing, your Nuk so close to me. Wherever I go there she would be too. Due to us having similar attitudes and views we were skeptical about trusting one another; however, I needed someone special to care for my daughter. I searched and searched and not one person I could find that I would entrust to keep my blessing. The day finally came when my mom told me that she believed you would be the best caregiver but in the back of my mind I said, "She can't be!" I prayed and waited and God confirmed it. I called you to make my request and ask your price and to my surprise you were extremely nice. You welcome the opportunity and with the rules you laid I knew our lives would never be the same. You knew of my early struggles and didn't want me to stress so you charged me little to nothing to care for my blessing. From the moment you cared for her an un-breakable bond was created. She was your Nuk and you were her Godmother Auntie Lena. I was your niece that you treated like a daughter and you were my Auntie Lena that I loved like a mother. Not only where you my aunt you were my other half, my confidant, my chastiser, my heart, my secret diary, my voice of reasoning and my friend. Who would have ever imagined two enemies becoming angels in the physical form? Through many of my darkest times in life you helped carry me through. There was never a moment you told me no when I needed you. I trusted you with my daughter's life; on many occasions when depression and sickness crept upon me you took your Nuk and kept her for weeks until I was back on track again. Often times I became overwhelmed with life trials and you helped bare my burdens making me face the reality. You stepped in the role where there was an absence and void that needed to be filled for my blessing.

    As I carried the role of single parenting there was never a time I called you and you weren't there for me. I loved how you never had a license to drive but you always made ways (having people chauffeur you around) to get to us. There was no need to list anyone else down for emergency contact because I always knew no matter if it's my job or Nuk's school you had our backs. In your privation of not graduating from school I was humbled that from infant years until it was time for school you willingly planted seeds of valuable morals, standards, ABC's and 123's. You planted so much so that your Nuk always prevailed as being an honor roll student and natural born leader. I admired you, your determination and your strength. You often shared your past with me and I could never imagine that pain being placed my auntie. I watched you triumph over the many obstacles that were meant to be stumbling blocks but the spirit within you made them into stepping stones or stones to throw at people. Auntie, you were one tough cookie! Anyone that knew you knew you were a force to be reckoned with. If it wasn't your attitude or disposition it was your mouth. Boy did you have a mouth on you! But, I respect it because no matter what we knew we would always hear the truth rather we wanted to or not.

Auntie you truly was the village that raised other people children. Although you may not have been rich nor had the finances to provide you was rich in spirit and much wisdom was instilled into those connected to you. There was never a dull moment being around you. You either were cussing or fussing someone out (including me) but most of all you prayed for us too. I never imagined you leaving us so suddenly. Years ago around the Christmas and New Year's season is when you became very ill and were hospitalized in intensive care. In that moments you looked as if you were going to slip away my heart cracked into pieces like a shattered glass never to be restored. I prayed for you constantly and petitioned God to raise you up from your sick bed. Several weeks passed then it went into months but the day you opened your eyes was the day I knew God heard the cries of the people that needed and loved you. We soon realized that although you woke up you were no longer you. I watched you overcome your health issues as you had to learn how to talk, walk, read, and write again. You had to do the very thing you often did for others which was to learn how to depend on others for help. You were truly a woman of courage, hope, and strength. You fought your way back sooner than doctors expected and you didn't let living with Chronic Obstructive Pulmonary Disease (COPD) and an oxygen tank define you.

    Life was back in place again and we loved living until that day came. The day when you called me and said you needed to have a talk with me about something very important. I became upset with you because you wouldn't tell me what the important news was at that very moment. When we finally had the talk and you told me that you were going blind, your breathing wasn't getting better and you would need two oxygen tanks instead of one, along with other diagnosis given by the various doctors you saw weekly. I said, "That's not a problem we can handle it we know God is a healer, besides you are a fighter auntie." I brushed the news off as if it was just another opportunity for God to work another miracle in your life. However, your tone was distant and unsure. Then you told me that the doctors said you only had six months but no more than a year to live. At that very moment it felt as if my heart stopped and I could not breathe. Numbness overtook my body and there was nothing but silence. When I finally was able to speak I asked you a million questions and only wanted the answers that I wanted to hear. It seems after that day as time went by I watch you become weaker and weaker. You would tell me that you were tired and the sickness was becoming unbearable. Every time the weekend, holidays, spring and summer breaks came as always your Nuk would come to stay with you. However, Nuk felt that those times were taking too long to come around so we begin to visit you during the week. Although we never wanted to discuss living life without you being with us you would give us instructions of what to do when the time came and you would no longer be here. We couldn't nor wanted to imagine it so we chose not to talk about it. Not long before your final days your Nuk stayed with you to keep you company, cook for you and administered you your medicines.

    I will never forget the day when I had to come and pick Nuk up and bring her home for a few days for a mini vacation but before leaving we all sat at the table and talked. Auntie, you begin to share your thoughts and give instructions on a list of things I was to do. You stated what I needed to do as Nuk was about to embark 7th grade in a different state; growing into a young lady; walking in the spiritual calling on my life; how to handle being a single parent with no or very little help; and being patient by waiting on God to bless with my husband etc. Afterwards you gave us both instructions of what to do and what not to do when you passed away. Although we listened very carefully we instantly changed the topic because we couldn't imagine life without you. If I only knew that was going to be our last sit down face to face conversation. If I knew that you were going to end up back in the hospital a few days later we would have let Nuk stay with you. If only we knew you were physically and mentally battling and things were getting worse; we wouldn't have went on vacation to Virginia Beach but stayed with you. I often beat myself up with what I could have done differently in hopes that you would still be here.

    On Wednesday August 13, 2014 I called you to fuss at you for telling me a lie about getting your smoke detector fixed.

You laughed at me and told me that the doctor just walked in and you would need to call me back. That was the last time I heard your voice. I waited for the return call and it never came. As I sat at my work desk and received the news that you were gone I couldn't breathe, I couldn't see, I couldn't think, I couldn't feel I felt non-existent. Life literally left me! Why God? Why would you do this to me? What have I done so wrong in your eyes that you would punish me this way? Who will be there for me? Who will I confide in knowing they have my best interest at heart? Who is going to help me raise my soon to be teenage daughter? These were the many questions I yelled out in anger as I dropped to my knees is despair. It hasn't been six months or a year yet. The doctors lied! It was just two months ago you told me the news. My life was forever changed. My everything has now left me with nothing! How am I supposed to tell my blessing that her heart in living form is no longer living? That was one of the hardest conversations I ever had to have. To my surprise Nuk already knew (in her heart she was just waiting for it to happen). She said during her last visit and stay with her Godmother Auntie that they shared their feelings for one another, and had a heart to heart goodbye if something would have happened before she made it back to her. Nuk knew she was very tired and ready to go home to be with the Lord. She no longer wanted her to suffer and go through life struggles any longer. So she accepted the death before the death happened in the natural form. It took my 12 year old daughter to put things into perspective for me. How selfish could I be to desire my aunt to be physically with us although she was in pain? However, I felt her leaving me so suddenly was selfish too. Her Nuk was about to start 7th grade in a week, her growing into a young lady was fast approaching; I just came to grips with finally accepting the call into ministry and you leaving me. How dare you! I had so many mixed emotions after my Aunties death that I didn't think I could manage to honor her request to read the scripture during her home going service. There was no way I could pull myself together to find the words to speak about the life of my Auntie. Only through the strength of God I was able to make it through that day and the days to come.

Often times while working I will burst out in tears and I would have to leave work. There are many days I go numb and many nights that were restless and depressing that you are not here with me. When your Nuk or I accomplish something positive or great I instantly pick up the telephone to call you as I would always do but soon realize you won't be answering. Periodically days come and go and I feel like I'm going crazy. I find myself talking to you and waiting for you to give me a sign that you hear me or just give me the answer I'm seeking instantaneously.

We are soon approaching the one year date of your transition that you left us but why does it still feel like it was just yesterday? My heart hurts, my mind is confused at times, and my feelings waver back and forth about your death but my love for you never changes it only grows stronger. I know without any doubt you loved me for me. You often told me how you were proud of me and all the things I do. I know you knew I felt the same because I told you too. How do I continue to live this life without you, without shedding tears when thinking of you., this I don't know? But I'm learning day by day that although you are no longer physically here with us your spirit will remain within us. The memories, your teachings, your laugh, your rolling of eyes while jerking your neck back and your "shugg" I will never forget.

Auntie, please never stop covering us, or sending your love from heaven above. You were given a new assignment to live in your mansion my angel my friend. I am assured that the life I have chosen to live now will allow me the day that I will see you again.

Words of Encouragement

Raven Simone

To whoever may read this book or my story I would like to take the time out now just to give you words of encouragement. As told in my story at birth I was diagnosed with sickle cell anemia, which my mother also suffered with and passed away from complications of the disease. Yes it was hard, and still is some days, not only with losing my mom but living with a condition with no cure. I have my good days and I have my bad, yes I get discouraged sometimes wanting to quit, but I serve a God named Jesus Christ and he is higher than anything that could ever come my way.

No, I'm not saying every day is going to be peaches and cream, it's not going to be how you want it always, but I am here as a living witness to tell you that when you put your faith and trust in God that anything is possible. If your heart really wants something go after it! No matter what odds are against you. There has been many times where I wanted to do things, or had goals for my life and was given negative reasons of why I couldn't. Whether, it was doctors, family, friends, people in school or just people in general. I've always been told I can't do this or I can't do that because I'm too sick. Oh of course at times I was discouraged and even thought why bother trying? But I never gave up.

After my mom passed away I graduated from high school in 2008 (on time), I went to college and graduated with a Associates Degree in Medical Assistant, and now at 24 I'm working on returning to school for my bachelors in Health Administration.

So with that being said, I pray that you go for the things your heart want and desire for YOUR life. I pray that with everything you do, put God first and put your faith, trust into God; he alone can do all things.

If you're like myself and have lost someone maybe your mom, dad, grandparent, spouse, best friend, etc. ;I want you to know that the pain doesn't last always, keep your head up and trust that God makes no mistakes.

I am so happy, grateful, and honored to be able to share such an important part of my life to help someone else out there who may have gone through some of the same struggles I have so, Thank You!!

Remember God CAN and He WILL! You too are an overcomer!

Let's Pray

My LORD JESUS, comfort your people. Strengthen the bereaved, hold the fragile, guide the lost and heal those broken. The loss suffered has been great and they feel like they can't go on, like they shouldn't go on. To move on with their lives makes them feel inconsiderate and disloyal ....help them to take the next step. Enable them to accept your will, and know that you did not do this to punish them. Let them know that they were left here to keep things going and not to lay down with a desire to give up. Help them to take their next breath, they feel like they can't breathe. Like they just can't make it......it's too hard......they can't do it.....they can't do this......they didn't want this..... JESUS....JESUS....come quickly! In JESUS name......AMEN!

~It's Not Until Death~

For our present troubles are small and won't last very long. Yet they produce for us a glory that vastly outweighs them and will last forever! So we don't look at the troubles we can see now; rather, we fix our gaze on things that cannot be seen. For the things we see now will soon be gone, but the things we cannot see will last forever.
2 Corinthians 4:17-18 (NLT)

"I Can See"

NaKyiah K. Nichols

I can open my eyes and see
All the many blessings God has granted me
I can open my eyes and see
How his grace favored and covered me
I can open my eyes and see
Oh there were many years of daily eye drops, and patching
That spiritually and physically drained me
I can open my eyes and see
How God believed in me
I can open my eyes and see
How he kept me and I survived through
My three eye surgeries from infancy
I can open my eyes and see
He blessed me from 20/90 vision to the 20/20 vision he gave me
I can open my eyes and see
So now I don't worry about what they say about me

Broken With Purpose

Monique "Poetic Rain" Favors

    A warrior was born in Miami Beach, Florida 35 years ago. In my heart, I believe at birth God gave me the gift of writing and poetry. He knew my words would speak volumes from all the life experiences I would later endure. At the age of 3, I was diagnosed with Sickle Cell Anemia an illness that almost took my life in my early 20's twice. Nobody could have equipped me for the life I was birthed into but God knew. I couldn't have been prepared for the childhood molestations from family members from the age of 4 until I was 11 years old. There is no way I could have known the impact it would have over the rest of my life. Even the domestic violence my father committed towards my mother altered the way I would view men and my future relationships. On top of experiencing the two date rapes, I endured as an adult left me wondering if I was only birthed for pain. However, my first rape before the two date rapes was very violent and committed by an ex-boyfriend at the time. This later led to me having an abortion. An act I committed that I still regret. Thank God for the forgiveness of self because taking his life haunted me for years. In the midst of it all, there were the many battles with illnesses that would soon consume my everyday life. Yes, God had to create in me a creative spirit!

    It was through my poetry I survived the storms of life as they tossed me side to side. Through my words, I escaped into places where nobody could understand unless they walked in shoes similar to mine. God understood what I needed most and he blessed me with the gift to cope with all my pain. At the age of 18, God blessed me with the gift of prophetic dance. I call this my most treasured gift from Him. When I dance something takes over me and all I see is myself and God. A daughter dancing with her Father! I have often used this platform to speak about my traumatic past. Many times, when I am asked to dance it is in the midst of a personal battle. Talk about worshiping your way to your breakthrough. My ministry of dance broke me through a lot of painful periods in my life. At times, I could not bear the weight of it all. So, I am grateful for such an anointed outlet that allows me to release it back to the Lord where it belongs.

    I became a mother at a young age. Birthing my daughter Trinity at the age of 18 and later birthing my son Malcolm at the age of 23. They are my miracle babies. I was told I would die having them, due to my illness. I almost did lose my life after the birth of my daughter due to the amount of blood loss. Nonetheless, I am still here standing on the very faith my mother and grandmother raised me on. However, there was nothing that hurt my heart more than finding out my son carried the very same genetic illness, Sickle Cell Anemia. God saw something greater in me than even I could capture with my own eyes. Not in a million years would I have seen myself on stages telling the painful truths of my wounded past. Yet there isn't anything more rewarding than walking off stage and having women approaching me saying, "I've been through that too." or "I have known you for years and would have never thought you had that kind of life." It just goes to show you that a book can never be understood by its cover alone. People often forget there is an author behind the words and the story goes deeper than what it shown on the surface!

    In 2005, I began having seizures. After ministering in dance at an Annual Sickle Cell banquet, I collapsed and did not regain consciousness until the EMT's arrived. Each time they revived me I was back out again. After being placed in a private room in the emergency department, the seizures began and they came back to back to back. I believe it was between 7-9 seizures and I was scared out of my mind. I had never had a seizure my entire life. Why was this happening to me? Why was my body failing me? I could hear all the voices around me, but I was stuck in my head and not in control of my own limbs. I thought in that moment. This is it. This is how I am going to leave this world. In a room full of doctors, nurses, and strangers who were praying over me. While the father of my child sat angrily upset that I messed up his schedule by having the audacity to get sick while he was doing me a "favor." Oh, what a hurt that was for me!

In 2011, I became a wife but when it came to dealing with my broken past it caused me to battle with Post-Traumatic Stress Syndrome (PSTD). It's the pain that you can't physically see, but it hurts just as deeply on the inside. I never knew how severe my history of sexual abuse and the violence of my childhood would affect my marriage. Between the severe depression and suicidal thoughts, I was spiraling out of control and rapidly. I was too broken to be a wife. I barely had enough energy to love myself let alone another individual in that capacity. I am thankful to God I went through two Christian based programs alongside therapy which helped me to heal from that broken past. God has made me whole again in spite of the loss of my marriage. I would not wish separation or divorce on my worst enemy but through my pain God birthed my ministry. In 2013, I started a marriage ministry almost 4 months after my separation. God gave me this vision in the process of teaching me how to become a better wife despite my own marital struggles. My broken and unhealed past had destroyed the solidity within my marriage. Now God is using everything that was meant for evil for His good. Exposing my pain is helping other marriages heal. I have such an extreme passion for God's will in all marriages. Despite going through a painful divorce, my pure heart for marriage has only grown stronger.

Amongst it all I mentor sexually abused teen girls. Helping these young ladies walk through their healing to bloom into the women that God desires them to be is very empowering. This is something I didn't get a chance to do. I love these teens dearly like they are my little sisters. They truly pull at my heart's string. God has given me my voice back and I declare I will not be quiet anymore! My words and my voice are my greatest power. I embrace it with humbleness and humility. This story is not just my story, but it's your story...IT'S OUR STORY! There is probably nothing you've been through that I haven't experienced first-hand. I encourage you to keep going because pain doesn't have to remain in your present if you bury it in the past!

Born into a Life Sentence: A Glimpse from My Cells

Raven Cassidone

    I hate the pain your bring me woken up at three o'clock in the morning with the hurt going through my arms, legs, and backs. You ruin my good days of happiness and fun with nights of sadness and needles. You're with me for the rest of my days like a best friend always around, but we fight over my body like my enemy always kicking me down. I love the amazing people and experiences you have brought to my life but I hate the ones you have took from me, how much your hard times and pain have made me stronger, grow into who I am today.

    I thank God for my fellow sickle sisters and brothers who are now some lifelong friends. The doctors, nurses, teachers, family, and friends call you Sickle Cell Anemia, but me I call you enemy the villain who beats at my body destroying my bones and organs, tearing up cell by cell. Why do you bring so much pain? The color red that is used to symbolize love and passion is the same color of my cells that are affected and to me represent hate and misery.

The Definition of My Sanity
Taylor Culmer

With each passing moment with
Every breath, sweet smile and beautiful memories
Lies and turmoil only I can see.
No one knows, no one can feel how my body feels, aches, scars, and bruises.
Bones and cells slowly deteriorating,
waking up with only my soul and faith to keep me comfort.
Beautiful I am, but the misery still lies within, the heart can never break, but my battle to survive remains.
With all the love and support the sickness can't bring me down, yet it still reminds me that mortality haunts me.
I remain undefeated, fragile but forever standing strong and fierce, despite the war that is ahead.

Believing Is Not Always Seeing

Mindy Rae Ellison

     Wednesday, November 26, 2013 is an evening that I will never forget. I worked that day. It was a good day. I can remember feelings of joy and elation. I was eagerly waiting for the Thanksgiving holiday to begin. I was hosting dinner for the family at my home. After work I stopped at the grocery store and purchased a few items. People who know me fairly well know that I am not a procrastinator and can be extremely rigid in how I like things to be done. Everything was set in motion. It was quite the accomplishment. I was prepared. After these finishing touches it would be ready, set, go and let the cooking begin. If you want to make God laugh, tell him about your plans. This is a quote from Woody Allen, I believe the original quote is an old Yiddish proverb "We plan, God laughs."
but you get the idea. Every time I hear this sentence now I laugh, I could always relate to it but not as much as I do now.

     At approximately 9:45 p.m. while watching a movie in the bed with my daughter, I experienced what I now know to have been one the most transformative time in my life. I lost my vision in my right eye. An eye occlusion or eye stroke can cause sudden vision loss. And I would soon be told that there is no cure. One of the ophthalmologists' at the internationally renowned Wilmer Eye Institute Johns Hopkins Hospital in Baltimore, Maryland after examining my eye and performing a myriad of test looked at me and said "I am sorry Ms. Ellison. Modern medicine simply has not caught up." After receiving the news of the loss of vision in my right eye, I began to wonder if my life too had been destroyed. Would I be unable to carry on with the things I loved with one eye? I had no way of knowing what to expect. My life had always been full, including reading, dancing, shopping, and interacting within my environment. How would I regain my life? How would I recover my activities of daily living?

What did that statement mean? This unexpected information was too much for me to process in the midst of my pain. What could have been said that was even more inflammatory than that? If I could wave a magic wand and get rid of either stroke or my blindness, I would not hesitate to get rid of stroke and my blindness. I remember repeating silently to myself "mirror, mirror on the wall". I wanted this experience to be a dream with a fairytale ending. Ending in an abundance of tears was my happily ever after. Suddenly without any warning my life as I have grown accustomed to has been changed forever. Adaptation was going to be a challenge.

During the past couple of weeks I think it is possible I've gone through a rollercoaster of every emotion any human being is capable of experiencing.

Through all of this one thing has remained constant. As each day has brought new and more unpleasant things to cope with, one thing has remained constant. Through all of this as my family members and friends have changed their reactions to my new journey on what seemed like an hourly basis, one thing has remained constant. At the darkest times when I felt only God understood my struggle and yet God seemed too far away, one thing remained constant.

I persevered somehow like a roller-coaster, my emotions ranging from very high to very low. After instinctively learning how to cope on day-to-day basis acting as if I could see things normally, I pretty much had people fooled until I got caught not being able to see or read something, which makes for very awkward moments, I felt humiliated like I wasn't normal. Couple all of this and add an aging single mother and woman in middle adulthood and the tumultuous menopause years. At times it felt like an emotionally combustible situation. I persevered still. Add being newly elected as chapter President of my sorority and the craziness of my personal and professional lives! Life has a way of transforming into what it should be.

The only thing that has been constant is the generously offered words of caring, compassion, and understanding support that I have found with my family and true friends. To my family, friends, Iota Phi Lambda Sorority, Inc. sorors and co-workers , there are just not enough words anywhere for me to tell you all what this has meant to me. After the incident, when I could not sleep because of the fear ripping at me, I got on Facebook and just read your posts. When I was feeling the days ahead are something I was not brave enough to go through, you were there being brave for me.

Thank you all for the private messages and postings of understanding and encouragement. Thank you for taking time out of your own busy lives to help me deal with everything that has happened in mine. Thank you for giving me a sense of perspective and proportion when I was unable to find it alone.

I believe deeply in the Holy Trinity. Whatever God has planned for my life I will accept with the same enthusiasm and optimism that has always defined who I am.

Monocular Vision does not define who I am or what I will continue to accomplish throughout my life.

Thank you to my Mommy (Peggy Johnson Ellison) and my daughter Brittany Rae Massey (Britt Bratt) for your daily support, care, love and comfort. Thank you to my three brothers Tony, Edward and Maurice for representing Daddy with your love and support. Thank you Daddy Albert Ellison for covering me in prayer from heaven. I know that you are with me daily.

My Christmas wish for all of you is that you are inspired by this message of courage and hope.

Believing is not always seeing. It is KNOWING.....simply knowing that we serve an awesome God and the best is yet to come.

My Attitude of Gratitude

Giving thanks should be an integral part of our lives. Psalm 44:8 says, "In God we have boasted all day long, and we will give thanks to your name forever." In other words, thanksgiving should flow from our hearts on a regular basis.

My new life and personal testimony....." Thankfulness should be a way of life for us, naturally flowing from our hearts and mouths." I have been so very truly blessed. Wednesday, November 26, 2014 will be my one year anniversary of my second stroke which caused me to lose my vision permanently in my right eye. I was so saddened and in a virtual shock that spiraled rapidly into a major clinical depression.

That morning when I awakened and realized that I had lost my vision I experienced a life changing moment that will always remain indelibly impressed in my soul and spirit. What was to become of me and my life as I knew it? I was just really sad. I was living on raw nerves and I knew that I had to do something, but what did I need to do. I prayed to God for answers and direction. Then it was revealed to me that I had to develop layers of new skin over a long period of time. I had to learn that you develop skin with time and by letting other people love and take care of you. I could not out run my fear and pain. I found myself stuck in this new life space.

Eventually I found this one thing to be true. When you are depressed you cannot think your way out of bed. You actually have to get out of bed. I had to crawl through it. My fears, my pain and my "why me Lord Jesus?" Am I ever going to be able to live in full confidence? Will I ever feel like the me I've come to know all of these years since my birth? Again I am presented with another life changing event. I mean after the death of my Daddy and my dear friend Andrew Jackson Jr. what else could I possible endure. But through it all there was one thing that I did know. I knew that God was not a punishing God. My God is full of love. Love shows up in so many ways. Even in ways that we can't identify and are completely unfamiliar with.

My friends and family members have a tendency to forget that I am blind in one eye. I guess that means I can "cover it up or fake it, fairly well. " It's a lifestyle change for me, I've learned to work with it, around it and sometimes just plain ignore it. Every minute of every day I deal with situations concerning my eyesight.

So as I go through each day from attempting to put my eyeliner on straight to reading the small print on a prescription bottle and trying to decipher distances with everything I see or grab is extremely difficult. Stairways and steps are difficult because I can't judge how high or low it may be or every time I reach to grab something from you, I may miss it entirely....you see, monocular vision does not see in 3-D at all. Judging distances can be quite entertaining at times. Although I can't see in 3-D, I am still stepping in those 3 inch HIGH HEEL SHOES! I constantly deal with some level of humility on a daily basis. Anyone who lives with a disability understands what I mean and the feelings that go along with it. Please don't misunderstand me; I am so grateful for what I do have. I know things could be so much worse and that there are people dealing with physical and mental challenges that are more severe than what I am living with.

Today almost one year later I am fully present in my body: my truth, my power and my weaknesses. Where your passion lies is usually where you will find your purpose. I am learning my purpose. I am passionate about life and love. So that it my purpose in this life. It's easy to love and give and feel happy and alive when things are going well and when things are not going so well ...And I'm All In. Thank you God for this gift of life......my special life. Life and light can come from partial darkness. Believing is not always seeing. You have to believe with your complete heart and soul. You have to believe that from your personal pain comes your god anointed purpose.

If there were a definitive path to happiness and success, everyone would be on it. I am going to keep standing, keep learning, and keep living. The beginnings to new and good things are always the hardest. But that is the operative word......BEGINNING. Thank you, God for giving me hope and light so that I can in turn bring hope and light to others.
I believe I have found God's purpose for my life. I will live and walk in my light of resounding resilience.

Now, almost two years later I am still riding on an emotional high that has brought back not only a new found confidence but an outpouring of life and passion to share my story. Life is an uphill climb, exerting our energies while facing situation after situation. Continue to put one foot in front of the other each day while stopping to rest and always be grateful for the smallest of blessings.

"No one can make you feel inferior without your consent," is my motto. Every person has a special gift that should be shared with the world. So this is my life, I do what I can with what I have been given and I wouldn't trade places with anyone! I pray that I continue to be blessed by God and that I can be a blessing to someone each day of my life.

Thank you to all of my family, Iota Phi Lambda Sorority, Incorporated sorors and friends who supported me and continue to support me.

Thank you to my special blessings from God Victoria Harrison, Sara Foster, Cynthia Sterling-Harley, Leslie Parker Blyther, Barbara Gray, Vonda Hayes, Susan Michelle Whitley, Angela Powell Hendricks, Dr. Doris Browning Austin, Sheila Mobley, Audrey Trueheart, Vera Hale Robinson, Floyd Majette and the late Gregory Wright Sr. Prayerfully and thankfully these are some of the people upon whom I rely to understand and encourage my unlimited possibilities.

I thank you Jesus for every trial, every test and every silent tear. I am grateful that God has blessed me with a Mother who is a praying mother and a woman of God. Mommy I love you.

To my daughter Brittany Rae Massey my Britt Bratt you are the book that I read each day and the four seasons of my life. I am so grateful that God has allowed me to share my testimony, and He has allowed me to see my first project completed. I know from personal that losing an eye is a seminal event. But I balance the importance of this loss with a believable you-can-do-this attitude.

The key to prayer is not in what you pray or see but having the faith that God is going to answer your prayer. Hebrews 11:1 tells us that faith is not in what you see, but it's what you hope for.

Let's Pray

WHY!!!!!!   WHY!!!!!!!   WHY!!!!!!!!

Heavenly Father, I come to you with a heavy heart needing you to lift me up out of this pit. I don't understand why, I don't want to understand why; I just want you to take this bitter cup from me. I don't want this to be how you use me. I don't want man to see me like this. I can no longer hide what I'm dealing with. WHY ME!!!! It's not fair. I don't see you in this. I feel plagued...I don't feel blessed. I feel empty cause the doctor said and the devil said, and the doctor said, and people said and these side effects and these thoughts and I should just end it now.....BUT I DON'T WANT TO GO TO HELL. Please heal me, please turn this around, and please change this diagnosis. Please make the doctor's word a lie. Yes you are a healer, yes you do love me, yes you can restore me, and yes you can heal me. Yes, I am healed in JESUS name, Amen!

~Let's Talk about Sex~

God is our refuge and strength, always ready to help in times of trouble.
Psalm 46:1

When you follow the desires of your sinful nature, the results are very clear: sexual immorality, impurity, lustful pleasures, idolatry, sorcery, hostility, quarreling, jealousy, outbursts of anger, selfish ambition, dissension, division, envy, drunkenness, wild parties, and other sins like these. Let me tell you again, as I have before, that anyone living that sort of life will not inherit the Kingdom of God.
Galatians 5:19-21

I Will Speak Up

Janie Williams Brown

    For today my words have awaken inside me, simply because I am stronger, able to speak them and dare to share my testimony. For years I was afraid to confront the sexual manipulation that violated my childhood. Largely because of guilt and shame and a small part because my one attempt at words were rendered untrue. In such cases it is easy for a child to assume that silence is better. Before long time has elapsed and the outcome becomes adults living in silence, building unhealthy relationship littered with fear, shame and lack of intimacy.

    The day of reckoning came for me, in that; I was forced to confront my past in order to move forward in my future. The dysfunction that had become my measuring stick was no longer acceptable. The determining factor was my super over protection of my daughters, stifling their right to relationship with male figures in our family and in the community. My unhealthy had become their unhealthy but not by (their) choice. One day in particular, I was so tormented by past memories that I reached out to a professional counselor. I'm grateful that I did because she helped me to work through the anxiety. She reminded me of the need to empower my girls by constantly communicating with them the difference between appropriate and inappropriate touch.

    By doing so, I have given them the power to say NO and to speak UP! They will live a life of equality because they value themselves.

No means No but........
Carolyn Terry

No one ever wants to have this conversation, why? Don't you know if we did a lot of us could have been saved from the sick sin of molestation, rape, abortion and promiscuity. Sex is something that should be enjoyable between a man and a woman, a lifetime of memories where something good comes out of it. I know we are taught that it should happen between married couples, but we all know that does not always happen, it can start as young as five years of age. Okay, so you got this look on your face saying to yourself what does a child know about sex at five years old? Glad you ask, absolutely NOTHING! This is where my nightmare begins. Innocent, no clue about sex or body parts if I be honest. What is on the minds of these perverted men? Sad thing about it is that the majority of these men come from our homes our own family members.

    I recall living with my auntie who was married to this man and as I type this I can see his face so clear, clean cut with sneaky eyes finding his way to me whenever the opportunity presented itself. This wasn't sex, this was oral sex, you heard me five years old performing oral sex on this monster and him on me. Where is everybody, why isn't anyone coming down here checking on me, why have you seek me out to be your play toy? Who do I tell? Who is going to believe a 5 year old? Like everything else in my life another secret untold. Now that I'm out of this house I don't have to worry about being violated by any man again. Wrong answer, the nightmare doesn't stop it only followed me to my next destination. Because I was such a difficult child in their eyesight, it was time to find new residence for me and now the penetrating begins. Little did they know my behavior was a cry for help and I wanted out!

    Now living with my aunt, uncle and two cousins, finally a real home where I can feel safe, at least I thought, not true. My junior high school years what supposed to be the happiest moments of my life, until life takes a detour for me? Oh, no not again, this cannot be happening to me again. Is there a sign on me somewhere that says up for grabs? Between 13 and 14 years of age this man wants it all and age means nothing to him. Never knowing when he was coming, I stayed in fear. In my mind what are you doing you have a wife that you sleep with every night why me? I hated their work schedules because she always got off later than him meaning whenever he was ready to play house he would find his way to me. You're probably wondering where were his kids, in their room and knew not come out. I never understood why my auntie didn't pick up on it, whenever she placed me on punishment he would take me off. This was his way of negotiating with taking me off of punishment because he knew I like going outside to play, this was my safety nest. You have no idea how many days I dread going home from school. Here again not knowing if anybody would believe me, no I didn't tell the teachers, just continued to be his doormat. Time to go, auntie not understanding my behavior, HELP I need to get out of here now! Move back to my grandmothers and now these experiences have left me feeling unloved and I need to be loved, because in my mind my uncles have taught me this is love. I met and fell in love with the man of my dreams only to run into another nightmare. He was physically abusive and sometimes sexual too. No means no, but wasn't always taken serious, in the midst of all these sexual encounters I am now acceptable to anything.

    These men have taught me that whatever I do with my body will get me the desires of my heart for free, only it wasn't for free. There are prices in life we pay for every decision we make. Once my body has become immune to these acts of violence it was all I knew how to survive. There became a time in my life that I began to use my body to get the drug of my choice which was cocaine. The more I used, the more I wanted, meaning the more I used my body to sleep with men and it was unprotected sex. Now earlier I mention that choices we make can cause some consequences and this was one of those moments where I was raped by six guys when I thought I was only dealing with one. When I walked in I should have known there was more to it then I assumed, but drugs don't allow you to think, act only. This is a situation I can't even report because I put myself in this situation so I had no one to blame but myself even though I said NO! But there was another time that I almost got rapped and not behind drugs, but because I was hitch hiking, this is what I mean about choices; I was able to get away. Oh and let me not forget about the men of the cloth, that's right the preacher man they weren't exempt, you had money you had me. So see sex has no identification on who, but we have the ability to decide who and when. Through all my bad choices, some of my own and some not, I had 11 abortions, from knowing who, some from not knowing who and some from my lifestyle. I felt no child should be brought into a world where me myself is not even stable. If you ask me do I regret it now, my answer would be yes, because I now have no children even after the two I did birth. The doctor was wondering how I was still alive; he told me after three I was endangering my life. It's just so easy to take precaution to protect ourselves from having to go and do these kinds of acts and then have regrets later on in life. My regret after meeting and marrying the man that God sent me, is we tried everything we could to have a child together even going through the process of fertility clinics, only to find out that I had no more eggs left to have a child. I felt bad and there were days I even cried about it, all because of the choices I made. Even in my drug use of unprotected sex I still live to this day praying that I'm not ever HIV positive even after 22 years of being clean I still fear that day. My advice to you is we are beautiful women created in the image of God and our body is our temple. No one get to defile your body or your beauty, let sex be something you experience that is beautiful and not your worst nightmare, the beauty that I did get out of these tragedies was my two children.

Royalty Lies Within

Mishelle Mungin

Let me introduce myself. My name is Mishelle Mungin; I don't come from a long line of famous people or a lineage of people with great power and influence. I was born to a teen mother and my biological father was a much older, married man. I saw struggle in my mother's eyes, although she never spoke of it. There was poverty all around, but I was never hungry. I suffered sexual abuse at age 11, by the hands of someone my mom reached out to for help. I felt inferior, dirty, worthless and ashamed. I battled in my mind for sanity. I knew there was more to this thing called life and I went on adventure to find it. My idea of that "life" was not worth the fight. It led to a devastating dead end of lying, stealing, promiscuity, and eventually heart break. What good could possibly come from a heart that's been broken? My answer was found in Psalm 34:18. The Lord is close to the brokenhearted and saves those who are crushed in spirit. I found life, an abundant life in a Heavenly Father that has an agape love. He became the mender of my broken heart. For that, I am forever grateful. Let me introduce myself. My name is Mishelle Mungin. I'm not famous, rich, or powerful. I don't sit among the elite in society; however, there is royalty in me.

The "Ugly" Duckling
Jo Shanique Henningham

This story begins long before my first sexual encounter, although it doesn't begin in my early childhood. I was very fortunate growing up. I began my academic career at an extremely young age at a prestigious preparatory school in my homeland of Jamaica. I participated in ballet, was an avid reader, and all around, a happy child...

This story, my story begins from my first day of school in the United States. I remember the school, Sea Castle Elementary School in Miramar; where I specifically remember being bullied relentlessly; for a plethora of things, from my short, natural hair, to my non-name brand clothing, to my accent. I remember being bullied so badly during my 3rd grade year that my teacher at the time had to address the whole class on the matter; but then again, "kids will be kids." Third grade was also the grade in which I accepted Christ into my life. Although I was raised in a Christian household, my relationship with Him wasn't truly my own, but rather my attempt at mimicking my mother's relationship with her savior.

Sadly, the bullying didn't end at the "kids" stage— it followed me straight through middle and right into high school. In middle school, for reasons I outline below, my already low self-esteem plummeted. I began striving for the acceptance of my peers more than ever; especially since my father, who I was very close to, had to work out of town, and sometimes out of state, due to the lack of jobs within his career field, Aircraft Mechanics. I thought I could gain acceptance if I was prettier. I remember begging my mother to process my hair with a relaxer, although I was severely allergic to the chemicals within that relaxer due to my eczema. This would make me feel prettier, I believed. I wanted to be liked. I wanted to be wanted. I remember rolling up the top of the skirt of my school uniform in order to make it shorter —sexier— I was only 11— I craved attention, specifically male attention. I even started wearing tops that would show the very little cleavage that I had, and I began wearing excessive makeup (which I was also allergic to). I needed to fit in.

When high school began, I had a reputation; fabricated from assumptions about my sexual status. I was considered "easy," even though I hadn't given myself to anyone yet. But that changed rapidly. By the end of my freshman year, I had my fair share of sexual partners, all of who I considered friends. I had also experienced my first rape—by one of those aforementioned "friends." I became heavily depressed and was experiencing suicidal thoughts. I reached out for help from one of the social workers at the church I was attending at the time, and she, with the assistance of the youth pastor, were able to help me tell my mom the news. I then filed a police report, began counseling with a psychiatrist, and was almost placed on anti-depressant medications. After a long summer, I began attending a different high school, but again, my reputation preceded me. I ran into some people that knew me and supposedly knew my story, and the rumors began again; more vicious and more personal than ever since they now had a legitimate backing. I was my own worst nightmare, giving them fuel for the fire with which they were burning me. I continued to sleep around. Pain struck again when I was raped once more; almost like a déjà vu... My grades were at an all-time low, and my GPA was a 0.9. For this reason, right after my 16th birthday in 2011, my school asked me to leave. They suggested that I enroll in an alternative school, explaining that this would be my only option if I wanted to graduate with my class year.

I started at my first alternative school, which was an OCLC (off campus learning center) almost immediately, and spent that year wasting my time. Here, I never had the opportunity to make friends; especially since I was rarely in attendance (I was always skipping class). By the end of that academic year, I only finished two credits of my required six. At the end of the school year, my parents decided to send me to another alternative school with the hope that I would finally achieve academically.

When I started at my final high school, the change was tangible. I was an immediate favorite of my teachers, all of who told me how smart and special I was, and how far I was going to go in life. I was excelling. Most, if not all, of my grades were A's and B's. But I was still too far behind at the end of the year to catch up with my class. All of the students that were in the 12th grade with me graduated, and I was still left catching up. By the beginning of the next academic year, I was so close to graduation, I could taste it. I was above the required GPA of 2.0, had 22 credits, and would be done before the end of the year. I would be officially graduating upon the completion of 24 credits in December 2012. But in order to participate in the commencement of graduates in June 2013, I had to return to the school after I was done in order to get fitted with my cap and gown, get details for graduation along with other small details. So by the June 2013 commencement ceremony, I was already through with my first semester at Broward College South Campus. A great accomplishment that I believe was to impossible a few months prior.

  College life hasn't been simple, but I am making it happen. In fact, just chose my official major of Africana Studies for my Associates Degree, and I am hoping to graduate within the next year. And although I haven't chosen my transfer institution as of yet, I know that I want to attend a HBCU. I am also certain that I will continue my community work through activism no matter where my life takes me.

  And as far as my Christianity goes, I am currently on a path to seeking deeper truths. Overall, researching my history guides me to a deeper understanding behind my true beliefs; and I hope to use both, Christianity and spirituality, to better myself holistically. I no longer seek acceptance because I am on the path to accepting who I am as a whole, and I like, scratch that, love, which I am becoming.

My Brown Boy
Janie Williams Brown

    Surely my reasoning for having an abortion was first that of selfish ambitions and second, fear of what it would do to my mothers' hopes and dreams for me. I was in college at the time, my second year in and I had been granted a full four year athletic scholarship. I was afraid I was not only going to lose my scholarship but also a chance at making my mother proud. I was home on summer break 1989 and had realized that I was pregnant, two months in. I did not seek my mother's advice, nor did I adhere to the father's wishes. It was a choice I made solely on my own. Somehow I knew it was wrong but I couldn't see beyond my youthful perception. I didn't know how I could birth, let alone support a child. The biggest mistake that I made was not talking to those who could have helped me to see things in a better light.

    I still remember that day lying in the doctors' office (alone) and him using what sounded and felt like a vacuum to suck the tiny boy fetus out of my womb. It's hard not to think that I forfeited a life, a precious life that I would have loved and who would have no doubt loved me. For years, I dealt with the overwhelming shame of what I had done. However, through a process of prayer, repentance and self-forgiveness, I am now free (body, mind and soul).

    At the time that I write this book my brown boy would have been 25 years of age, a handsome young man no doubt. In his memory, I share this experience with you (my daughters' biological/mentees) in hopes that you will always make wiser decisions in your youth than I did. Never Lose Hope, Seek Light.

Little Sister

Tia Parker

Why do you think you have to sell yourself short; Lying with these guys while Gods plan you abort? When you say no I guarantee if he really wants you he won't leave. Ladies listen to what I have to say and take heed. Guys love to chase! And the only reason you want to do it is for him to be up in your face? After you give it up he will no longer be interested in you and every time he sees you all he'll want to do is screw. So you're going to give it up, sacrifice your life and your health? Suppose you get pregnant, have a baby you think he's going to be there to help? Suppose you get an incurable disease, you think he's going to fess up to it? Naw he's gonna say, "You ain't get it from me!" God sent me to you on divine assignment to say, if he cannot love you without sexing you, tell him to get out of your way! Please don't make that decision to give in. So what all of your "girls" are doing it! Ask them how many times has that guy hurt their feelings?

Sex without the union of marriage is so empty. You need some proof? I'm here just ask me. I am where you are if you look close enough at me you'll see my scars. See I'm wounded because I wanted to fit in with fake friends who were telling me how "good" it felt. Ladies, can I tell you after I did it I felt so filthy I was in a living hell? Sex without the permission of God is so meaningless and it leaves you with this huge void.

The only beautiful thing that I got of it is now I am a SINGLE mother to the most precious little boy. Now don't look at me and say, "Well oh at least I can get that." No baby I had to sacrifice a lot of life goals and it took a while for me to get back on track. So Princess just listen to someone who has just a little more experience than you; our God wants us to be virtuous women not fools. Just say NO!

Just a Form of Godliness: The Inner Struggle

Charlene Barclay Nensala

Sexin' him on Saturday
Goin to church the next day
Said my prayers in order to take the guilt away
Now he says he wants me to come over for another stay
God it's hard to focus because this brother is too fine
OOOps I slipped again, guess I'm gonna have to go to the back of the line and repent yes for another time.
Just another form of godliness you say but I don't see it that way can I at least get some points for repenting today?
We grew up together
Said we'd be best friends forever
Often wore each other's clothes and shoes
Would finish each other's sentences when no one else had a clue
Now she's found Mr. Right
I know I sent a text yesterday but still no reply
Said I was happy for her but I knew it was a lie
Now all I do is talk behind her back
Telling others that her dude is wack
Jealous maybe, but this goes beyond that
Truth is all I really want is my friend back
Guess I'm gonna have to go to the back of the line and repent yes for another time.
Just another form of godliness you say but I don't see it that way can I at least get some points for repenting today?
What's wrong with a little taste every now and then?
I can quit any time it's not like I depend
I know it's wrong but at least I'm not as bad off as the rest of them
I promise I'll atone in the end

Guess I'm gonna have to go to the back of the line and repent
yes for another time.
Just another form of godliness you say but I don't see it that
way can I at least get some points for repenting today?
I know Lord you said that you want all of me
Your will is for me to devote myself completely
Friends laugh when I get back in that repentance line
Pledging my allegiance to you for the thousandth time
When the truth is I subconsciously can't wait to get back into
my old rhyme
Just another form of godliness you say
I keep claiming I don't really see it that way
PLEASE HELP ME TO REPENT FOR REAL BECAUSE I KNOW
THERE'S GONNA BE A JUDGMENT DAY

Oh How I Wish

Minister Tanya L. Baylor

All I would hear momma say is, "Finish school first then you can have a baby." I didn't have the best childhood growing up but I didn't have the worst either. I just knew as a kid that some of the things that I experienced and seen growing up I wanted to do the total opposite. I wasn't raised in church but I often heard my grandmother talk about it when I would take summer visits to the country year after year. My grandmother didn't take me to church with her but she made me and my cousins learn Psalm 23 by heart. She would tell us that whenever we found ourselves in danger or trouble to always repeat Psalm 23. Throughout my adolescent and teenage years I kept two things in mind which were to finish school then have a baby, and repeat Psalm 23 whenever I was in danger or trouble. Often times I look back over my life and oh how I wish I had been taught what I now know about having a baby. I wish I had someone to pour wisdom into me about the importance of remaining a virgin until marriage. I would just repeat Psalm 23 when danger and trouble was near but, I didn't understand the importance of believing God's word. I wish I had someone to teach me about accepting Christ at an early age while living a life that was pleasing unto him.

Needless to say all this was just wishes because at the age of 21 I considered myself a numb human disposal of innocence. What does that mean you ask? Let's say I did finish high school with honors and college receiving my Applied Associates Degree in Legal Studies graduating with Magna Cum Lada Honors but I never had the babies. Yes, babies! I did exactly what I was taught and I didn't think anything was wrong with how I was living and allowing my body to be tainted, used, and abused out of wedlock. I was a numb human disposal of innocence (unborn children) times five. It's ironic because now that I am saved and accepted Christ as my Lord and Savior as soon as I hear the number five my mind automatically thinks of "grace" which the number symbolizes in Christianity.

    Prior to me truly desiring to live the life God called me to live when I would hear of the number five instantly I would mentally go back to the place where I begin using different names and locations for my disposal because I didn't want the employees in the doctor's office to remember me from the time before. I didn't want them to recognize that I was there again and assumed I was using abortion as a form of birth control. All four (I had the nerve to become pregnant multiple times by the same man) men that help me conceive but did not accompany me nor did they financially support the cost of the procedures. Therefore, sacrifices had to be made. I was a full time college student and full time employee but had to find ways to save extra money for the procedures.

    I remember the very first abortion I had numbed me. I blocked it so far out of my mind that I returned to my daily activities and way of living right after I left the doctor's office. As soon as I left the office from aborting an unborn baby I went shopping for baby items as a gift for a baby shower I was attending the next day. I acted as if it never happened and in my mind it didn't. I continued on with life never allowing the thoughts, sounds, pain, and after affects taunt me as if often tried. However, as the multiple procedures begin to progress I found myself mentally becoming unstable when seeing children in public that would be the same age as mine if I had chosen to have them. I found myself having on and off depression spells because when it came to my sexual promiscuous lifestyle I could never make the right choices. I would allow my non-chalant attitude and lustful desires to overtake what I felt in my heart were wrong. A few times I remember feeling very faint and light headed hours after the procedure and I would wonder if they left any parts of the fetus inside of me. I was bleeding so heavy that I wondered if I was hemorrhaging and no one detected it. The pain pills they prescribed weren't helping. Instead of the pain going away it seems as if it became more intense. While battling with the mental stress and physical pain I would pray and ask God that if he would stop all the depression, stress and pain that I was feeling I would never have another abortion again. Yes, then the next time came again, then again and again. When would this lifestyle of being a numb human disposal of innocence stop? The day came when I found out I was pregnant and I didn't have the desire to have my fifth abortion. The thought never entered my mind and it was because I had begun attending church more often, reading the word of God and desiring a closer relationship with Christ. I finally started realizing that I was destroying the temple (my body) I was blessed with and I had to learn my self-worth as a woman. Although, I wasn't perfect and my sins allowed me to fall short at times I was determined to no longer allow my sexual, lustful habits, and promiscuous lifestyle dictate me making life changing decisions that would haunt me mentally, physically, and emotionally. It was a blessing to be a mother of such a beautiful baby girl. Deciding to have my daughter changed my life. I was determined to be the best mother she could ever desire to have. It was my unconditional love for her and my desire for her to have the best life growing up in Christ that I vowed to teach her the things I longed to learn growing up. Although, her father and I never married I embraced being a single parent knowing that God was our Jehovah-Jireh providing everything that we needed.

    Life seemed as if it was beginning to fall into place for me until four years later it happened. Yes, I became pregnant. However, my feelings, thoughts, and behavior towards being pregnant were different than before. I was involved with a man that was soon to be my husband but in my heart I knew I couldn't live a lie nor live the happily ever after I often dreamed of. I was searching of a way to leave an abusive relationship and remain gone without desiring to ever go back. I then popped up pregnant; this is the worst timing I thought to myself. During this time I could only remember how I desired to please God and once again I let him down. As days went by I constantly pondered on having the baby only because I didn't want to let God down once again; however, I knew within my heart I couldn't bear the thought of a baby growing inside of me that would have me connected to such an abusive man for the rest of my life. The emotional, physical and mental abuse I was enduring at that time was the determining factor of me being a human disposal of innocence once again. I became so determine to have an abortion that I talked my doctor into allowing me to have the procedure done at five weeks instead of the normal eight week timeframe. I hid the pregnancy and abortion from the father until weeks after it was all done. I knew he desired children being that he had none of his own and he would try everything within his power to prevent the pregnancy termination. Having this particular abortion opened my eyes why it's recommended that you be eight weeks pregnant before having the procedure. The risks are greater such as: having portions of the fetus being left inside of you; damage to your inner uterus walls while causing the inside pelvic area and tissue to be tender; excruciating pain and uncontrollable bleeding. Because of my decision (and to this very day) I experienced all of these risks with the exception of portions of the fetus being left inside of me. I laid on that table with all these symptoms and blurred vision looking at the ceiling with tears running from my eyes asking God to have mercy on me. That day I vowed that I would never allow myself to be in that type of predicament again. This specific abortion opened my eyes tremendously reminding me that negative consequences will be the result of making bad choices and being disobedient. This lifestyle is one of many that that taught me the lesson that although people can offer advice, assistance etc. the ultimate decision is mines and I must be able to live with the consequences rather they are good or bad.

  To this very day nine years later I've kept my vow, but as I look back over my past I say to myself, "Oh how I wish!" Oh how I wish I could turn back the hands of time when I was a teenager and young adult but what would that matter? In the situations I allowed myself to be in I would still have disposed of the five innocent unborn children that I was carrying. Why? I was clueless about the life I was living and the decisions I was making. I believe I did the best for me at those times. However, those experiences of lack of love, knowledge, and teaching have helped me become who I am today. Oh how I wish I could turn back the hands of time of when I was an adolescent and young girl but what would that matter? It would have mattered because I would haven't looked for love in all the wrong places; I would have been aware of my self-worth and not let men and situations short change me; I would have been determined to remain a virgin saving my precious gift until my husband found his good thing; I would have known its more to life then finishing school then getting pregnant and reciting Psalm 23 when in danger or trouble. Oh how I wish when you young ladies hear the number five you instantly think of "GRACE" because it's a gift of unmerited divine sanctification, virtue, pardon and special favor to us from our perfect God.

A Fool for Boo-Boo

Lakita Stewart-Thompson

Always having a sense of hope, I found ways to simply cope
I cried, fought, and sometimes I just gave up and gave in but
God always seem to wrap me in his arms and hold me, wiping all of my tears of way
I got up as if everything was completely okay
But really not so
Only to find that years of my life had been repressed
I was just go comfortable entering circumstance after circumstance undone, heavily stressed
I was stripped naked but I supposed I got undressed
I always felt like I meant more, but my mind kept telling me I was less
As I sat down in the comfort of my inner most feelings I began to assess me
I realized that my heart had been broken for such a long time constantly
I never knew how much baggage I carried around from past hurts that regulated every aspect of me emotionally, spiritually, mentally and physically
Disappointment after disappointment, hurt after hurt, bouts of unexplainable pain, I felt like so heavy
The bricks of life rested on my back, quiet easy
Fixated, planted so deeply
Enduring the repetitive cycles of bondage of simply existing
With the spirit of heaviness, depression and failure which birthed much insecurity,
Now loneliness and unforgiveness arrest me
I constantly felt lost abused and confused
I began falling over from the weights of adversity, all suppressed in multiple bags, thrown over my shoulders by the enemy
I was weak and life was meaningless
And then a tainted love found me.

Though a wretch, my love was stretched and his name was Boo Boo.

    I remember my very first time ever running away from home. I was about 7 years old. I remember hitch hiking and getting into strange cars to get away. Simply trying to escape from a painful place where nightmares haunted me every night. Not feeling loved or wanted. So I was going to create my own love, no matter what. Never knew why but as time progressed, I buried some memories as deep as I could but noticed they began to rise as I tried creating relationships. Carrying so many unresolved issues but I became a fully functional, dysfunctional human being, I lived a life of chaos and no boundaries.

    Now here it is my fifth time running away, and I am old enough to catch the Greyhound! Well when I met Boo -Boo, I was 14 going on 30 and thought I had it all together. I was Mrs. Mature with a capital M and figured I knew best. He was a relative's boyfriend. But being young, dumb, and naïve little me, I didn't know what was evidently inappropriate if it smacked me in the face. Back then we were taught that anyone older than us was considered aunt or uncle out of respect, no matter what the relationship. He said he would be like a big brother look after me. I called him uncle out of what I thought was the respectful thing to do. During this extremely rebellious stage in my life, I gladly accepted he proposal as kin. He also expressed his concern for me in more ways than one. He would make sure I was going to school, making good grades etc....He said he wanted to see me excel. So checkup phone calls became long hours on the phone after midnight. Mind you he is an older relative's boyfriend who is somewhere in his late 20's and little o' me 14 going 30, thinking I had it all together. I began to not only talk to him more and more, but seeing him on a daily basis. Some days I never made it school. The conversations began getting personal and intense, but in my mind very much innocent. This was a time in my life where I also began experimenting with alcohol heavily and attempted smoking. We began drinking and smoking often. In his eyes I was the safest around him and my family when it came to experiencing anything, considering he was my so-called brother/uncle. He promised to never harm me or allow me to be harmed. So I trusted him. I mean no one else would help me.

    Before the blink of an eye he began giving me soft innocent pecks on my cheek as he dropped me to school. Low and behold I found myself really liking the contact. It never dawned on me to think beyond the surface of it all. I mean, I do like him. He has become very much helpful in my life and I need him to survive. He makes me laugh within. He is oh so attractive. But he is my relative's boyfriend and I think I like him. I think he likes me too.

    One evening Boo-Boo came over to spend time with family. We all played cards as usual, had a few drinks and even a great meal. Well I decided to leave for a few and go to the pay phone to talk to one of my home girls because cell phones weren't in during this time. To my surprise, Boo Boo followed me. As I stood in the phone booth, he approached me asking me to open up the door so he could talk to me for a minute. As I opened the door, I could smell the strong aroma of his breath. His strange behavior immediately was an indicator that he had one too many drinks. I found myself in a struggle to get him from trying to pull down my pants, unbuttoning my shirt and forcing his hand in my sacred places. I screamed as loud as I could possibly scream, dropping the phone. He began forcing his tongue in my mouth. I fought with all my strength and was easily dominated. He insisted that I wanted him and I was playing and flirting with him and he wanted to give it to me. I raised my knee as high as I could and tried to hit him wear it hurts only to be choked nearly to death. All I could hear was some banging on the outside of the phone booth. But I was too faint to open the door. It was only by the grace of God; someone recognized me and came to assist.

    That day really changed my life and I blamed myself. I put myself in that situation knowing it was wrong. Being taking advantage of and attacked by someone I thought I knew was something I never imagined. It was devastating. All I could remember in my mind was my father's words, "I don't care where you go, there is no place like home!" From that moment on my life was never the same. I was tired of running from my problems and being violated in the process. I was tired of trying to find myself. Tired of looking for love in all the wrong places. Tired of living a life of uncertainty. Tired of near death tragedies. Just tired.

I thank God for sparing my life so many times. I returned home, finished high school, college, went to Africa, and taught at risk youth. It was in my teaching experience where I was able to assist other children who too had similar issues with their identity that I learned a lot about myself and my purpose in life. Through my negative experiences, I was able to help children find hope and love themselves.

All things do work together for our good. We have to understand that what we go through is never for us, it's to help and save the lives of others. It's all for God's glory. He will never give us too much to bear and our stories have value.

Therefore, I encourage the youth reading this that have to endure even greater challenges than I, to put God first, pray always, and surround yourself with positive people who truly care about you and have your best interest at heart.

Your life does matter.

"The Divine Gift"
Torri Rodgers-Ball

If I had the wisdom and knowledge that I have now when I was 15 years old; I would say to you and my younger self that your "Divine Gift" is special and should not be taken for granted. "The Divine Gift" is your VIRGINITY. Making the life changing decision to lay down with someone who you will possibly never see again, break your heart, cause you mental turmoil, and/or never marry is very serious. Your GOD given gift of virginity is a sacred trust that has been given to you to have and to hold until marriage and not to be given or taken lightly. Every person felt the peer pressure and curiosity to have sex; however, you can WAIT! It is special when you have matured, in love, and married to your husband that GOD has sent to you.

If he can't wait; he wasn't the one perfect for the cake! There aren't many discussions on a Woman's virtue but, I believe it's time to not leave our younger generation hanging by them. Sex is not a light conversation to have nor is it a topic to take lightly, opening yourself to sex, boys and men, leads to the discussion of Sexually Transmitted Infections Diseases, unplanned pregnancy, confused emotions, and unwanted attention from your peers. To be honest, everyone is not having sex; I understand that it is easier said than done. I would say to you, focus on your education, travel, and hang with people (peers) that have your best interest at heart. Love yourself more and not dishonor your gift that was given by GOD!

Let's Pray

Almighty FATHER that sits high. Great is your mercy towards me, thank you for the love and kindness you've shown me, that you would spare my life for this very moment. You didn't let rape kill me, or allow molestation to destroy me, and you didn't allow my misuse of my flesh to stop you from wanting to use me. Great is your mercy towards me. Thank you JESUS. Thank you for not letting me die in depression, self-worthlessness, self-hate, self-torture, shame, blame or sin. Rather than condemn me you rose for me and has since snatched me from the burning hell that desired my soul. My GOD....thank you, in JESUS name, Amen!

~Why Daddy~

Even if my father and mother abandon me, the LORD will hold me close. Psalm 27:10

Me
Kalia Foster

Deep inside of me a troubled girl cries for peace
To get rid of all the lies and pain
That at one time helped her sleep
The lies helped her sleep because she thought they were the truth
And the pain made her numb so there was nothing else to do
Like a whirlpool of rumors
Words are all she can hear
She can no longer make them make sense
All that lives inside her is fear
She never had his guidance
Her first love turned his back
And they had the same DNA
So what hope is left in that?
He was supposed to lead the way show her what a pretty girl deserves
But neglected that responsibility
So his little girl took some wrong turns
Left alone to make corrections
To decipher genuine from fraud
To decipher her worth and those unworthy
Of her beautiful yet broken heart
Her dream is to look in the mirror
And see happiness in her own eyes
To be strong despite the tragedy her heart has learned to despise
Forget the fact that her father neglected her and never made an attempt to turn back
Or the struggles she faced with her mom
Who damn near broke her back
She had to grow up so fast
Put on some armor just for show
God forbid anyone find out
That she's usually at her low
They make fun of her as it is
Not knowing what she's faced

Not knowing that she's always wished to be normal
Moving at their pace
Her writing is her only escape
Like therapy for her soul
Her release
Her raw feelings
A gift God gave her to grow

Absent

NaKyiah K. Nichols

An ideal family is a father, mother, son and a daughter. As for me my life was never like that. It has always been me, my mom and my cat. My mother has been my sole provider. She is the one that takes care of me, make sure I have everything I need and want. My father was what I would call absent. He is living but never around although we only live thirty minutes away and our churches are side by side. He is the type of father who some would call non-active. In my opinion my father partially took care of me, nor did he ever have a true father and daughter relationship with me. For example, we don't have good or consistent communication nor spend quality time together. Although we never had the relationship I desired I never disowned or disrespected my father. It never really affected me until I became older. I begin to find myself being hurt or feeling some type of negative way. He would always say, "Let me check my schedule," or "I'm going to get back to you" whenever there was a school function, church event, or when I simply asked to see him or hang out. Anytime we spoke it would be because I called him.

My father has five children. I have four brothers and I am the only girl. I can honestly say I have only seen him take care of one of them, which is my youngest brother that lives with him. Honestly, I look up to my brothers more than I do my father. Everyone on my father's side of the family including his church family and friends always says he's a good man. But, aside from being a good man, it takes a real man with love, patience, and humbleness to be a father. My dad may be a good man but is he a good father? Is he active in all his children's lives (I'm not talking about just child support checks)? Nevertheless, I feel that my dad had it easy. He didn't have a negative or threatening baby mother. My mother didn't ask for much if she asked for anything at all. I can only recall my mother only asking for him to be a father. I used to try to talk to him and about him as less as possible. Until I had to realize at the end of the day he was only going to be my biological father weather I wanted him to be or not. Then I remembered that my father named "Jesus" filled in every void that my biological father didn't fill. Nobody would ever know my story because no matter how frustrated I got with my father you would never know unless I verbally told you. Somehow I always managed to have a smile on my face because of my father and me knowing that one day I wouldn't have to worry about my dad and the wrong I believe he did. One day someone shared with me that they were in the same situation growing up and that it would be okay because I had my mother. At that time I really didn't understand how it would be okay and that God was going to be my father no matter what until late 2014. When it comes to my father, I hope for the best but expect the worse. In doing this, it has helped me to cope with my father being "absent." If I don't have an expectation nor get my hopes up high I don't have to worry about being let down or disappointed.

    It wasn't until June 21, 2015 on Father's Day when I was thinking of writing a letter to my father expressing how I felt. I felt the least I could do was send him a text message saying, "Happy Father's Day" since I didn't purchase him a gift. However, when I begin to type I felt the need to express my feelings at that time. I expressed things to my father that I had been holding in my heart for a very long time. Once I sent the text I didn't know how to feel. All I know is that I finally told him. My father responded stating, "One day I would know more but until then just pray for him." Later that day my mom drove by his church and I asked my little brother to tell our dad to come outside. My mom, dad and I had a very long intense conversation that was initiated by the Father's Day text. During the conversation we expressed how we felt but most of all how we were going to change something's moving towards the future. We acknowledge that there are some things that needs fixing and we talked about how that can be done. At this point I am open to whatever God has in store for our father and daughter relationship. I believe there will be a day God is going to work my situation out completely no matter how hard it gets. Now I just have to pray, wait, and hold on to my faith. I would say to anyone who has father issues to be encouraged and always trust God.

Filling the Void
Raiya Coates

My father and I DON'T have a relationship. Growing up without a father is one of the hardest things that I have ever had to cope with. When my father left me and my mother when I was 2 years old and decided that women and his career were more important than his child it broke me. My father did have me once in while he would take me to his family's house such as his mother and sisters place. My family members saw me in a different way. Cousins on both side of the family boys and girls put me under complicated circumstances. It was a lot of sexual secrets between me and them growing up. Boys would want something from me and so did the girls. If I didn't keep my mouth shut about it, they said that I would get in more trouble. So I just always did what they asked.

My mother was in search of a mate and sometimes that would hurt me because I felt that she would do the similar things because she couldn't handle being alone. Her mate searching seemed like it was more important than caring about my feelings. I didn't grow up in a poor neighborhood or was abused by my parents, but my parent's actions, emotions, and mentality is what hurt me the most. Boys begin to come around and I lost my virginity in the beginning of my 7th grade year.

I started to do what my father did which was have relations with multiple boys and care nothing about their feelings. I would have sex with them and leave them. My body was never a temple. The more I thought about my father having his 6th child and my mother having her 2nd child. I hated and resented them because I felt as if they didn't understand why I was so emotionally damaged. How could they think to bring another child in this world. On top of that I felt they didn't understand that every decision that they made would also affect me. In my eyes their children didn't come first. I went to high school and had therapy sessions and they didn't help me, so I smoked more, I gave my body up more. I wanted to cope. My grades were never consistent. But by the time I hit the end of my senior year, me and my father bumped heads even more. He told me that he didn't even want to see me on prom day or graduation. I was fine with that but I couldn't believe that he would ever admit it. Now I'm in college and working. I'm majoring in criminal justice. I was requested for an honors program. I have consistent grades and I slowed down on my recreational activities a lot. I have showed that I can overcome my feelings and that I will not let them run my life. There is so much more to come for me.

A Yearning for You

Lakita Stewart-Thompson

Yes, I had a two parent home and everything
I needed in your eyes.
From mine it takes more than you simply being able
to provide.
With no hugs and I love you's
just distance
feeling ignored.
I often fell into the arms of the enemy because that
is the place I felt most adored.
Lived a life holding most of your secrets and lies
so, I went from a broken little girl to an angry, bitter,
and bruised woman.
Wounded by the pain I felt inside
I guess your love for me somehow died.
Trying to figure out what, when, where, how, and why
Trying to understand why you favored kids not even
your own and simply passed me by.
Tried to let the favoritism within that was blatantly
obvious just ride,
I remember sometimes feeling loved but most of the
time denied.
Felt tolerated, felt a strong sense of your hesitation to
love me.
As if my life on earth was created mistakenly
Always ask myself what I did to deserve this rejection,
I always felt from you.
I guess I should be grateful at least you took me in.
But, why do I feel more like a stranger off the street
rather than your kin.
Never felt that love I was looking for, just been suffering.
It's been hard to find love because my heart has been
heavily aching.
Simply standing by the side of your heart waiting

No matter how hard I tried to fill this void,
there's really no replacing
my love for you can never be questioned or
mistaken.
Little boys and little girls need you in every way.
May seem like everything is alright
but, we are really not okay.
A hug, kiss, some quality time, or I love you isn't
really hard to say.
I remember God soaking my tears and I just
began to pray.
Society can now raise and love your children
without even being in the home.
Even more so with the creation of iPad, social
media, and cell phones.
Parenting is dissolving more and more
I know it isn't easy.
Just want to be noticed by you, appreciated, and
happy.
I've learned that Christ is the true keeper of love
but, sadly I really just yearned
for more of your love.
There's nothing like you affirming me that I am
more than enough.
But the longer I live the more I realize
to not put my trust in any man, but to keep
my eyes focused on Christ.
Who paid the price and made the sacrifice,
who shed His blood for me and loves me
unconditionally.
As I reflect, I am learning to just accept
the path that Christ set for me.
It's time forgive, move on and live freely
love as Christ loves and cast all my cares above.
By His Stripes I am healed
All the pain, hurt, is sealed.
I understand without you I wouldn't even be
here
And I love you with all my heart.

Healing Is A Process
Kimberly Nicholson

Healing is a process. In no manner, shape, or form can one skip this process because it is essential to an effective God-centered Christian life. Sometimes it takes years to heal because our hearts cannot let go out our past hurts. But we must understand that complete and total healing is possible with God. We must understand that God is a Healer and He can and will do it for us if we want Him to. However, it is a process which you have to make the conscious decision to participate in. At a very young age life's unfavorable circumstances left me with tremendous heartache and pain. I never thought that I would forget the little things such as: his touch, his smell, his kiss on my cheek, or his love. Yet, all I can seem to remember is the fussing and fighting; the cheating and the stealing; the lies and the backstabbing; disconnected vows between the two people I cherished the most-my mother and my father. Somewhere deep inside, my heart tries to remember my father's smile that always seemed to brighten up my day; my father's hugs that seemed to relay to a sweet, innocent little girl, that everything was just fine; and the kiss on my cheek which signified him always being there for me. But somehow my mind just can't seem to fathom what seems to be an internal fantasy of mine. Truth is, all I remember is being the happiest little girl on earth, and then one day I woke up and I was all alone. The fussing and fighting, the cheating and the stealing, the lies and the backstabbing had all run their course; the man that meant the most to me as a little girl was gone- my father. And with him went my hopes, dreams, and aspirations.

When others look at me they see someone who appears to have never had struggled. They see someone who's too young to have gone through any real trying times. They see someone who is doing well and appears to have no heartache or pain. Yet they are so wrong. You think I haven't been through anything? You think because I'm only 28 years old that

I haven't experienced life to the point where I didn't want to live? You think because I have my own car, appear to be paying my bills, take care of my three year old son, work full-time, and attend school full-time, that I haven't experienced anything? You think the smile you see on my face every day is always sincere; always there because I'm always blissful? Well let me tell you something... I wasn't raised in association with any Hilton ancestry heritage; I didn't get anything on a silver platter. If anything, I had to try and make my own spoon. Therefore, you are sadly mistaken. Every man I have ever loved has walked out of my life with no apologetic feelings. I grew up in a single parent-family; poverty was my generational curse. I had an abortion my senior year in high school which created feelings of worthlessness. So called friends walked in and out of my life. I had sex just to feel voids within myself. I was afraid to really trust and love anyone because I had been hurt in the past. I had more bills due in one month than I had money coming in in two months. I had a car repossessed and my credit went downhill. Many days and nights I starved so that my son could eat. I hated my father for leaving my mother with three children. I tried to overdose on pills because I was hurt and upset. I felt hopeless, and worthless, and empty. I was told that my life was over because I had a child and was not married. But yet I haven't been through anything? Oh no, you are wrong. I had to endure just like everyone else did. Yet, God didn't let me go.

You see, God knew before I was even born my purpose, my call. In all my mess, in all my heartache and pain, He came to see about me, always providing protection. I could try and take my life all I wanted to, but like Dr. Yvonne Capehart out of Pensacola, Florida said during here message titled "Dream," "When you are anointed, you can't abort it....you don't have the power or the authority to stop the plan God has on your life." She was exactly right. No matter what I did, God had to come see about me because He had chosen me from the beginning. He sent Obedience to me and said watch over her because when it's all said and done she will come knocking on your door, ready to serve you; ready to obey; ready for her divine healing. I'm not perfect and I still have things that I am working on, but I serve a God who refuses to let me go and is always near, here, and there. Daily I am learning what it really means to be healed, to be free, and to be an inheritance of my destiny. This day, make a stand. Refuse to be a slave to your heartache and pains. Process what needs to be processed, take it as lessons learned and knowledge and wisdom gained. Then ask God to help you let it go and watch miraculous things unfold right before your very eyes; watch true healing manifest.

My Cross

Monique "Poetic Rain" Favors

Daddy, it hurts...

I'm trying to hold this cross but this pain won't escape me
I've tried to stand on your word in the midst of his hate spree
Pushing myself above these aches that keep on trying to break me
Taking up my cross appears to be too much but it's carved into my destiny

Daddy, help me...

I don't want to move out your will so I'm trying to be still
However, I admit if I could I would like to numb what I feel
It's like I'm drowning in this sea of red from all the blood that I've spilled
Every time a wound tries to close the deeper the cut goes and I can't seem to heal

Daddy, I'm heartbroken...

Like shattered glass from a broken mirror I've been exposed
I can't hide what was done to me because it was publicly disclosed
A tactic by the enemy to destroy my new formed identity of being whole
Attempting to assassinate the character of the woman who prays daily before your throne

Daddy, it's me...

Standing in the need of your prayers
Like an onion this healing it comes with many layers

I need you to intervene on my behalf because at times this pain I cannot bear
But I know that this pressure builds praise so I refuse to take off running scared

Daddy, save me...

Rescue me from these lies where love once resided
Sometimes what looks like the truth can be so one sided
I wish all of this pain I could contain but I just cannot hide it
Therefore, I allow my words to bleed onto this paper until the ink runs dry

Daddy, wipe my eyes...

I want to stop from crying but my soul feels like its dying
I feel like he just reached into my chest and snatched out my lifeline
Killing me softly with the illusions of you'll never see me in the next lifetime
I'm trying to wrap my mind around this mess but they keep saying, "Moe it's just a test."

Daddy, I need you...

Help me to understand why must I endure so much?
At what point, at what time does my pain finally reap the benefits?
Please, Daddy tell me that there is a greater blessing on my life after this
I'm trying to be strong, I'm trying to hold on, but I need your help with this

Daddy, I trust you...

Even though my heart it hurts like hell I'm right here
I 'm holding up this rugged cross that feels too heavy to bear
I won't come down Daddy until you release me from my despair

I know it's bigger than me, I know you're using me, so for You
I'll hang here

Daddy, I submit…

I lay all my pain at your feet in humility
And I even thank you for using this pain to humble me
From the outside looking in they can't understand the truth I bleed
But that's okay because I'll be the sacrificial lamb so your glory is achieved

Daddy, I thank you…

I'm grateful that you listened to my silent cries
While tears flow from my eyes I still find the strength to rise
Thank you Daddy, for knowing I was strong enough to be stretched out
Although this pain pierces through my flesh nothing but your love will pour down

Let's Pray

Yes JESUS loves me for the bible tells me so. Thank you LORD for loving me when daddy walked away, after he promised to be here, he still walked away. When after he laid eyes on me and saw that I was perfect he still walked away. Even after hearing my innocent cry, he walked away but YOU walked up just in time. You caught me just before I fell. You stepped in right on time. Thank you for giving meaning to Father's Day. It's because of the love you've shown me that I'm not bitter. Thank you for taking away jealousy, envy and resentment and replacing it with fulfillment. In JESUS name, Amen!

~You're Expected to Win ~

As the Scriptures say, "For your sake we are killed every day; we are being slaughtered like sheep. No, despite all these things, overwhelming victory is ours through Christ, who loved us.
Romans 8:36-37

Each time he said, "My grace is all you need. My power works best in weakness." So now I am glad to boast about my weaknesses, so that the power of Christ can work through me. That's why I take pleasure in my weaknesses and in the insults, hardships, persecutions, and troubles that I suffer for Christ. For when I am weak, then I am strong.
2Corinthians 12:9-10

Just Like A Lemon I'm Being Squeezed

Charlene Barclay Nensala

Just like a lemon I'm being squeezed
All I wanted was a life of comfort and ease
But you said you had different plans for me
Now day and night all I do is beg for peace
Your response to me was my grace will provide sufficiently

I'm often, compressed, depressed and even possessed with rage. I feel as if it's just too late. Seems like the victory you promised is past its' due date. Lord please help me not to faint

Just like a lemon I'm being squeezed
All I wanted was a life of comfort and ease
But you said you had different plans for me
Truth is I can feel you slowly replacing my once roaring
spirit with your stillness as I wait on you patiently

Your Holy Spirit keeps telling me just you wait. I reply the manna I'm receiving while in this wilderness is all fine and great, but I'm ready for other options on my plate. I often feel as if it's just too late seems like the victory you promised is past its' due date. Lord please help me not to faint.

Just like a lemon I'm being squeezed
All I wanted was a life of comfort and ease
I know you're taking the sour juices out of me
You said you had different plans I see
Transforming within me a new spirit that is sure to
please……

But my flesh is still torn because day and night all I do is beg for peace

Ironically in spite of my pain, I can also feel your Shekinah reign

The more I try to pray my way out of my current state, it seems like you place more obstacles in my path just to keep me behind this gate. I know you're a jealous God so you'll do whatever it takes to keep me humble divinely packaged as my fate.

Just like a lemon I'm being squeezed
All I wanted was a life of comfort and ease
But you said you had different plans for me
Now day and night all I do is beg for peace
Your response to me was my grace will provide sufficiently
I THROW UP MY HANDS AND BOW MY WILL TO THEE

My Mistakes Became My Testimony

LaShonda Renee Alexis

My name is LaShonda Renee Alexis and I am 33 years old. I am the mother of Brandon age 15, Kai'Asya age 10, and Antoine age 6. I am a cosmetologist by trade, but a logistician is my career. I am also a successful entrepreneur. I got married in December 2002 and was divorced in November 2009. Since then I have been a single parent. I graduated college in October 2013 and am now working on my bachelor's degree in business, concentrating in the area of supply management. Now, God has given me the assignment to help young women by telling my story. I built the organization/ministry called Dazzling Divas empowering women towards success. My vision is to MOVE. Motivate young adults to Overcome obstacles, Vision success and Embrace change. This is who I am.

As a child I was never a part of the hip crowd. I had friends and they were always very nice to me as I was to them. I wore glasses and I had braces throughout my middle school years and got teased, A LOT! I grew up with two parents in my household, my mom and my step-father. Although I did have two parents in the house it was my mom that ultimately kept the household going. Sometimes I would ask myself how she does it. There was always one thing that stuck out to me that she would always say and that was stay in school, get a good education, and never put yourself in a position where you have to be dependent upon a man to take care of you. I thought she was going crazy and just wanted me to listen to her fuss all day long. Back then I truly didn't know what she meant by that, but what I did know was that I better finish high school and go to college because she would kill me if I didn't. What I didn't know was that she was molding and shaping my way of thinking so that I could be Bold, Strong and Confident.

At this point, I'm a senior in high school and I knew this was going to be a great year! My family always said, "Oh Shonda you're so smart; you're going to be successful; you've done more than what we could have done so no excuse you're going to college." My plan was to graduate high school, go to college, and land the career that would make "my family" feel like I made it and I was successful. The key words in that last sentence were my family. They never really asked me what it was that would make me strive for success. I was always a demand that I will or I won't. Well sometimes it doesn't always work out that way. Now I would say it was the devil that threw a monkey wrench in my good plans of life, but God will allow certain things to happen to us and shake things up in our lives to get our attention and to draw us closer to him. At the age of 15, I was secretly dating and boy that I had met while I was on a school field trip and we dated for years until he graduated and left to go into the military. I just knew I was so deeply in love. He and I started having sex and we knew it was wrong but we snuck around to do it anyway and I got pregnant.

I was a senior in high school in JROTC and chorus holding very high positions within these organizations and pregnant. I couldn't go to my friends because the entire school would know. I thought to myself who am I going to tell about this? I surely can't tell any of my family and I was afraid to tell the teachers that held me to the same standard as my family, if not higher. I just didn't want to hear the words "I'm so disappointed in you." I wanted to get rid of my child, but God was not going to let me off that easy for being disobedient. I went through 6 months of lies and hiding until one day my mom said she was taking me to the doctor because my sister snitched on me. I still acted like I didn't know what she was talking about and she made my life very miserable until I had him. She didn't act like that because she didn't love me; she did it because she really loved me. She was starting to prepare me for being a mother and woman. She still focused on my education and made it clear that it was still my number one priority, but I had to focus for myself.

Ladies we get so concerned about what everyone else wants we can't find our own light. You must be able to locate your lighted path. Only God knows the plans that he has for you, so you have to sit and have a little talk with Jesus. When I became strong enough to understand that my dreams didn't have to be mom, dad, brothers or sisters, I gained the confidence to have a voice and stand for what I truly loved. In finding my voice and my path, I still didn't learn that I had to create positive energy.

When I look back I can honestly say that I had lots of positive people that were in my circle of influence. When I was in high school I had positive teachers that spoke life and success over me. They were just like mother and father figures, but nicer. I can clearly remember Ms. Jones my choir director never use the word 'try because' it's just like saying I can't or I won't. She taught me how to have correct posture from siting straight up to sing and most of all she taught me not to be afraid to chase my dreams. She made things happen for us as children that most adults would never do in their lifetime. My JROTC instructors groomed me as well. SFC Kinzer was not just a teacher but he definitely was a father. He actually asked to be my sons God Father and that he was. Now pay close attention to how God set me up for success and showed me my path. He taught me the basics of the logistics and running a supply room for the military long before I thought about making it a career. Maj Dunmyer another father to me was another instructor.

One day, we were just standing around and he came by each of us and told us what we were going to be doing when graduated and he told me entrepreneur. Years later a retired instructor convinced me to volunteer at the school because they needed a female to help with the female cadets. I accepted and became a voice that the young ladies in the program actually listened to and learned from.

Now, let's go back. When I graduated high school I chose to go to Cosmetology school instead of college and graduated. I then enlisted into the military working in the logistics field as a Unit Supply Specialist and I also work it as a civilian today. Then, I met a young lady that introduced me to owning my own business with Mary Kay Cosmetics and I have been doing that for 8 years. Now, I am sharing and motivating young women to strive for their absolute best. I'M not saying that you should be disobedient but see, God had his hands on me and guess what? Although I didn't follow the route my mom wanted me to take nevertheless she is still very proud of the woman that I have become and my success. God is an Awesome God!

Stand

Anoved Sivad

When the devil loses his grip and control
He lashes out like a child as His world unfolds.
Using every tactic
every trick that He knows...seeping through the cracks of even your home.
Stand on your faith and never let go...
Know your rightful place and what's in your soul.
Need not complicate for the truth He'll soon behold.
Your Father sends Angels with wings
Unto You they hold.

"The Power of Influence"
Shaniequa L. Washington

Shaniequa L. Washington born to a mother who did crack cocaine and lived in government assisted housing in the Bronx, NY had a future beyond the statistics of welfare and poverty. It gave me the ability to reach for the stars and to trust in a God that would do exceedingly above all I asked for or ever thought I could ever be which back then was not who I am today. I have been given the opportunity to break barriers in corporate America in being an African American female leading a team of over 300 people daily in a male dominate market. I have been called by God Himself to lead and to influence and inspire women across the world to grab a hold of the vision that they are different and they have been called to be set apart and to be Holy and to lead with integrity and honor that they are who God says.

If I had not been influenced I would have been discouraged, discouraged by what I experienced, what I saw, what I felt like I could have never achieved thinking I would never be worthy of any cause because I was a cause from a situation that looked as it had no worth. Influence in my life allowed me to influence in my mom's life. I am so proud to say that my mother is clean of drugs and alcohol and she leads in ministry over the drug and alcohol ministry helping people to cope with issues of life leading to an abusive life and influence them to seek God and open their eyes to see, if God did it for her that He will do it for them. Influence is a gift if used in the capacity for which is designed, which is to develop which means to create what once did not exist.

According to God's perfect will this would be for greatness. Habakkuk 2 tells us to just live by Faith. Habakkuk 2:2-4 tells us "Then the Lord answered me and said: "Write the vision and make it plain on tablets, that he may run who reads it. For the vision is yet for an appointed time; But at the end it will speak, and it will not lie. Though it tarries, wait for it;

because it will surely come it will not tarry. Behold the proud, His soul is not upright in him; But the just shall live by his faith.

As a leader influence is the most powerful tool that you have to lead a group of Individuals into a place called success from a place once called undeveloped. Influence what is it? It is the capacity to have an effect on the character or the development, or behavior of someone or something, or the effect itself. The words that resonate with me are the ability of strong leaders of faith is the effect itself. When leading from a place of total influence it should have resounding effects that goes beyond the common place but taps into the paths and dimensions that man in it just could never do. To develop is the process of developing or being developed. This means that you and I must always be open to the necessary molding and prepare to mold someone into a place called destiny.

The journey........ I recall in 1997 coming into what I thought was a part- time job and simply living to work until I was developed to work to live. I was molded into an individual who learned to build on precepts and principles that builds foundation and allow paths to be made. I started for one of the largest corporations of the world as a cashier and found once developed that with God and development that nothing was impossible and all things are possible with God. In 2000 my journey soon began. I moved into various hourly supervisory positions which allowed me to be trained and molded by individuals but there are two are three that I will never forget because of their profound words of wisdom and firm ground of development and always seeking right direction that helped me develop strongly in my work ethic as well as sparked a total interest in spiritual development. I found myself yearning to attend conferences for development from a leadership prospective as well as a spiritual prospective not knowing that influence lead me to a place of faith and professional growth. In 2008 I was asked by a human resources manager to participate as a speaker at a woman in leadership seminar and speak on mentorship and what an awesome topic I found to expound on since influence had a great part in designing and cultivating the individual I have become. By 2006 I was offered a position to become a store manager of a 70 million dollar facility and broke ground in creating history as the first female and first African American female in the particular area I was asked to lead in. This was a great moment of influence as I soon had women from all walks of life seeking from me the secrets to my success. This is where I saw how powerful influence can be and recalled all of the influence I experienced and the path it created for me.

   The Vision...................... Influence created the vision to see myself in a place that I have never been, to experienced and had never seen. Influence showed me there is more for me than average but that there is a path that has been created for me. Influence showed me that in my being peculiar that it would awaken others that are different. Influence sparked interest and awareness of what is available and accessible to me. Influence said when you can see, you can know that I am more than a conqueror and I am above and not beneath. Influence gave me vision.

What lies underneath

Charlene Barclay Nensala

And by the looks of things, it seems like they're living a life most of us can only dream.
I see him in his shiny three piece/ hair brushed nice and neat/ others bow as he takes his seat/ and by the looks of things/all of the bling on his ring indicate he's living a life most of us can only dream.

Excuse me sir, if you don't mind me asking, may I peel off a layer of your life/I'd like to see how you really handle anger, jealousy, and strife/When times get tough do you fall on your knees and go to your secret place/or do you attack everyone who comes into your space?

I see her in a couture gown that's very picturesque/Out of all who've showed up to this event she was voted most likely to succeed and best dressed/Shiny teeth, hair styled nice and neat/others bow as she takes her seat/ and by the looks of things/all of the bling on her ring indicate she's living a life most of us can only dream.

Excuse miss, if you don't mind me asking, may I peel off a layer of your life? Are you passionate about a particular cause/or would you rather spend countless hours on the phone discussing idle thoughts/ How about the true reason behind that success/ are your life's choices really the fruit of what God would co-sign as blessed.

I see them exiting their parent's car/ His starched pants, her pleated skirt, their Ralph Lauren polo tops/ They sit at their desk arms placed in a fold/ "Always do as you're told little ones, don't be the first to break the mold/Heaven knows you have your parent's legacy to uphold/" What lies underneath is what I often wonder/Don't you want to mimic daddy's success or mommy's beauty and land on the front of a magazine cover?

Ma'am, sir, and little ones; may I peel off a layer of your life? How are things going in your home/Was dad sober enough this time to leave you alone/Did mom threaten his life the next time he touched another woman who wasn't his wife/How about the payment on the house note/I noticed your family has a tendency to unplug the phone.

    What lies underneath all these people I've had the pleasure to observe and meet/From the outside, it looks like they're living a life most of us can only dream/ Is it heaven, is it hell, or a combination of both/ yet they choose to show the world only the parts that's accepted by most?

    By the looks of things, it seems like they're living a life most of us can only dream.

Overcomer Is My Name
Shalonda "Treasure" Williams

It is never just enough that an individual makes it through their storms or their tough times. That is the glorious part; the part we get to shout about and laugh about. The most difficult part, for most, is finding the strength and courage to be able to speak out about the challenges and all it took to *overcome* so that someone else can have a chance as well. It takes a boldness to speak out the things that we did in shame. It takes much heart to be able to look guilt and embarrassment in the face and tell it to "BACK OFF... I HAVE TO DO THIS." It is one of life's most selfless acts. Yet it is scary. But it must be done. So I speak this piece as an *over-comer*!

The word *overcome* means *to get the better of something*. When it comes to emotions, according to bing.com, it is to overpower or overwhelm. Doesn't it just sound so awesome to think of overpowering your emotions? Guess what? It is absolutely possible and it can happen for you. Just like me and so many others, being an *over-comer* can be your status for today and every day. Let me warn you... It takes work. Intentional steps and intentional decision making. It did for me.

Catch Me! I'm Falling!

One of the greatest, biggest and baddest challenges to get pass would be an enemy called depression. Another would be bouncing back from a setback such as homelessness. One more would be rising from a stigma that says, "Now no one will ever want to marry you with that many kids." Yet, I have taken all of these things and took charge of them. As a matter of fact, I took a big bite out of depression at the age of 26.

There is nothing like the embarrassment of being a "church girl," in the middle of writing and publishing a Christian book and then you fall weak. Falling weak from not saying no to temptation. In this case I had been celibate for a while and I was content not having a man in my life because I was so thirsty for God. I was at church every Sunday and at every bible study on Wednesdays. I was not just going through the motions either. I was truly hungry for the teachings and I was growing so much. I loved singing in the choir and on the praise and worship team. Life was good.

At this particular time I had allowed one of my friends from school to come live with me for a while. She and her son needed a place to go. It was only right, in my heart, that I should let her come home with me. We were great roommates. We had no problems. We used to talk all the time. She felt comfortable enough to bear her soul with me and I was honored to listen. I would wake up in the mornings with such a pure joy in my heart. Singing and praising Him early in the morning as I walked around the house was my norm. It was a great place and time in life and all was well.

My new roommate was very close to her family, especially her brothers. They used to call her almost every day. She would speak about all of them and their lives. She made mention to me that all of them were attached except one. I really brushed it off at first because men were not the center of my focus. One day, however, I heard her talking on the phone. She was answering questions and they all seemed to be about me. "Oh, that's Shalonda, the lady I'm staying with." "She sings all the time and yes she does have a beautiful voice." "Yes, she is single but she's like me right now. She is not doing anything with anybody." "Why do you want to talk to her?" It was kind of funny to hear but as always I begin to tune it out. One day out of the blue she says to me, "Are you open to talking to anyone? The brother that I told you was single wants to talk to you." At first, I am like OH BOY! Here we go. She went on then to tell me that he was a believer and about his bible study habits. I begin to get intrigued so I agreed to talk to him.

Talking to him was one of the easiest things ever. We clicked right away and it was beautiful. We did this for about 3 weeks, talking on the phone every day and every night. He was living out of town so I was excited when he told me that he was getting ready to visit. We just knew that it was going to be the best thing ever. Needless to say, when he came to visit, all the saving of myself that I was doing was no more. It went out of the window and 3 weeks later when I missed my period I knew that I was in trouble... AGAIN!

Baby #4 was being formed in my belly. I was sick as ever and even more depressed than that. I did not resist temptation and now I was living with the results of that. Not only was I pregnant again but I was ashamed. I felt so convicted that it hurt to open my eyes in the morning. Here I was about to have another child out of wedlock and I was not even totally in-love with the father. We were getting close but finding out that I was pregnant changed a lot. I became so irritated with him that I pushed him completely away. He even asked me to marry him and I said no. I was a mess. This was probably the lowest depression I had ever experienced. I even considered getting an abortion. This was something that went against everything that I believed in but I needed to cover up the shame of what I had done. Get rid of the evidence of my fall and go on like it never happened. Yeah right! I was selling myself a lie.

The lie was big, but the weight of it all was worse. *What is everyone going to say? I know that Pastor is going to be so mad at me. No one is going to buy a book from me like this. You are a big hypocrite.* This is the self-talk I had going on. I just knew that my life was over at 26 years old.

Life had such a cold feel to it. I was alive but barely. I could not eat from being sick, but even if I could I would not have because I wasn't hungry and food was nasty. I think that my children ate more cereal and hotdogs then than they ever have or will because I had no energy to stand up and cook. No one outside of my home saw me for a full month. The only reason why my mother saw me was because she had a key to the house. I did not want to talk on the phone. I would keep the blinds and curtains closed all day long. I wanted no light to shine on me. There was nothing bright about my situation. This was not baby number one. This was not the first time, second time or even the third time that I had gotten caught up in this kind of situation. Wasn't I supposed to be stronger than this spiritually? Why could I not get it right for once?

The reality was that I was hurt and disappointed with

myself because I had failed at the task of keeping myself until marriage. I had finally gotten a great momentum and I was working it and here comes a man and I ruined it. *Dang Shalonda. Are you ever going to be strong enough to date without messing up? Are you always going to give in to those lustful desires? Will you ever get it right?* The disappointment that I felt toward myself I let pull me deep into a place of "I don't want to exist anymore." Now, was it the end of the world that I was pregnant? No, absolutely not. However, I felt it was.

The Bounce Back

I was lying on the couch about a month after finding out that I was pregnant. I was still depressed and still confining myself. I had not been to church in weeks and did not plan to return until after the abortion was done. The baby's dad and I talked it over and had agreed that we would go half on it if that was what I really wanted. He didn't want me to do it because it would be his first child and he was still willing to marry me. I was just not in the frame of mind to think of that as a possibility. I had a Christian book coming out soon and there was no way that I was going to go through with this. I guess I could have married him and tried to cover it up but I could not really stand him at the time. He had not really done anything negative to me. It was just that he was attached to the situation; a situation that I wanted to go away. I checked my child support card and it was just enough on there for me to get the procedure done. I thought that it was meant to be the way that money had shown up.

On the couch that day I was watching TBN and crying. Pastor Rod Parsley was on all that day talking about abortions. *How odd is this?* He goes on and on talking about how wrong abortion are and how God would not be pleased with it. I cried even harder. I watched and felt convicted, yet I was still carrying all the shame and guilt that was attached. So, warning or no warning, I picked up the phone and called the abortion clinic and made me an appointment. I was to report the next day at 10:00 a.m.

I was numb but something in me kept me watching TBN. I had not opened up my mouth to pray in weeks and I had no interest in doing so. But, about four hours later my phone rings. *Pastor Rouche'* is what the phone said. He had called to see where I was. "I don't hear that holler over there in that corner." Of course that is when all the dams broke. I cried and sobbed and told him everything. After telling him there was this long silence. *I didn't come because I didn't want you to be mad at me.* "I'm not mad Shalonda, but I am disappointed. But, no matter how I feel about it, I need you to know that God still loves you and so do I. It happened now it's time to get up. I will see you at bible study Wednesday."

Needless to say I was back at bible study that Wednesday. I was there but not there. I just could not stop crying and all eyes were on me or so I felt. I was not even showing yet so they didn't know. But, I felt the eyes of the world staring me down like they knew my inner most, darkest secrets. It felt like a pit.

I have to admit, it lifted a bit of the weight being in a crowd of people that could give it to you straight but still walk in love with you. I was not completely there but it was a seed planted. But, before I knew it I was trying to slip back in my shell. I got home and was over taken by the spirit in my home. I was ready to curl back up and close the blinds when a knock came at my door. It was one of our ministers. This sister was my mentor from afar. She was bold, beautiful, anointed and powerful! I admired her a great deal. When I opened the door there she stood with this big grin on her face. "Let's talk in the car Girlie." We did and I know to this day that she was strategically placed in my life to shatter my pity party! Like CRASH! Within that conversation with her I gained so much relief and I laughed so hard that there was absolutely no way I could turn back around. She laid it out for me, but it was up to me to choose to take the bait. What kind of bait? The bait that caused me to *overcome.*

I overcame Depression

This was probably one of the darkest times of my life. But it is only one story amongst dozens of stories of me dealing with depression. It has camped out with me for most of my life. The difference between now and before that night is that I felt powerless to stand up to it and win. Now, I stand tall within myself and I know that whenever it wants to rear its ugly head I have the power within to knock that head clean off the body. There are a few things that I learned that I will share:

- No matter how big the fall God cares enough to help me up if I simply ask Him.
- There are times when I will be the target of a formed weapon, such as depression, but the power of my words and my actions are unmatchable when done in faith. (The enemy gets nothing here).
- Life is not over until it is over. As long as there is still breath, there is still time to start again.
- GOD'S GRACE IS SUFFICIENT! PERIOD!
- Everyone has a struggle, we just have to know that we can resist. It may take effort but it is possible.
- I can throw away shame thinking that everyone is pointing fingers. The only difference between me and some others is that I got caught because the evidence of my fall was there for all to see. No one else is so clean that they can cast the first stone.
- I still have a purpose! I cannot ever let the enemy think that he is so powerful that he can change or cancel the plan of God for my life.
- When I begin to fall into a pit, I must actively take a role in bouncing back. Sitting idle makes me prey. I must get up, take action, by walking in nature, listening to uplifting music, feeding myself some word, watching or listening to something empowering or watching a comedy on T.V.
- I have the power to overcome this thing called depression. I will not let it win and neither should you!

Where is Love

Kalia Foster

She smiles
But fears behind it
As well as sadness
There it dwells
She wonders if her eyes show it
Or her voice
When she speaks
Her emotions swell
She tries to run away from them
All the questions their faces ask
But how would they understand what she feels
If her emotions she unmasked
Nobody likes rejection
To feel ejected empty and hollow
She's fallen plenty of times
But the heart of another never truly followed
She dreams of a love so deep, so revitalizing so real
One true love for a lifetime
Pain from all the past concealed
If only she could forget all the nights she couldn't sleep
Holding her pillow tight as the tears
Shamelessly drip down her cheeks
She catches them on her lips
Wishing only for a kiss
Like one she's never had before
Could one truly fathom this?
Everyone longs for the idea of love
but for others it's in every step
in every breath they take
True to form
in life itself
will she ever win?
Will just a snippet of her fairytale come true?

If she closes her eyes and wishes
will she open them and see "you"

Give it to Him
Anoved Sivad

We often ask God "Is it His will?"
And wait to hear Him agree with what we feel.
We really don't want to know what He wishes; instead we hope our desires appease what he teaches.
We seek the Lord but only to a degree. We need to surrender to him and then we will see. Surround yourself with likeminded children, and then you'll have no choice but to yield to Him.
Seek Godly council to sift through your situation.
Everyone isn't of His Holy Nation.
In the multitude of council there is safety.
Don't just take one person's word and become hasty.
Stop going to people that will just agree. Find those that will help you genuinely. Those that are friends can also be an enemy unintentionally.
God's will isn't always positive, and there's actually some good in the negative.
In this life you will endure pain. That's the only way you can recognize progress. He isn't always an "either or" God...but sometimes multiple choice, giving you the opportunity to use your voice.

Hey Young Girls The World is yours!

Monique Price

Hey Young Girls yes you! I know that sometimes you may feel like no one see's you or knows you're alive, well it's not true. People are paying attention to you more than you know. Yes some may be looking at your assets and your most attractive features; however, some are just watching you bloom.

Dear Young Girls of the world, I'm writing you this letter to inform you that the world is yours. If you've ever listened to a rapper named Nas; not only does he say it he also believes it. See with this kind of thinking you're bound to reach great heights. Harriet Tubman I'm sure you've heard of this famous slave who helped free several other slaves with the Underground Railroad movement she said that, "Every great dream begins with a dreamer. Always remember, you have within you the strength, the patience, and the passion to reach for the stars to change the world."

Hey Young Girls, I want you to know that anything you want to achieve in life is possible no matter how hard it looks. Thomas H. Palmer who was an American educator in the 1800's and is most famous for the quote, "If first you don't succeed try, try again." These are powerful words to stand by in whatever you do in life.

Being a young girl in a cold world is a challenge within its self and the fact that you were born is your first blessing! You have a responsibility to provide the world the best of you. There is nothing greater than you because you are capable of bringing new life into the world. Hey Young Girls, take a moment to think about that. You will be a part of birthing a nation. As you grow you will have many and several hurdles to jump but don't get discouraged for it is all there to make you stronger and to create the person you were destined to be.

From the words of the great late poet Maya Angelou "all great achievements require time."

I know each stage in your life you have a craving for something, it could be having friends; getting good grades; being popular; having a love life; wishing your parents understood you; wishing you had good parents; understanding your purpose; wanting to be beautiful; wanting a better life; wishing you were someone else, or just wishing God was really listening to you!

Well girls I'm here to tell you that you will have friends that come and go for reason and for seasons, you will achieve whatever your goals are as long as you put forth effort; your parents Over-stand all that you go through; the parents you were giving will be a part of your journey for growth; ugly ducklings always turn into beautiful swans; the life you want is obtainable with persistence; as you grow in life you can be that person you desire to be, and GOD is always listening to you just pay attention and you will be able to see that.

So what is it mostly that all the young girls in the world should know? Hey young girls that you are beautiful no matter what anyone says and you need to believe it for yourself. You are beautiful no matter how society defines beauty and to love everything about yourself or no one will, Gabby Douglas USA Olympic gold medalist said, "Don't be afraid to speak up for yourself and to keep fighting for your dreams!" So you shouldn't be afraid to dream big and follow through with them, Know that the pain you experience in life is your purpose, stand firm in what you believe and let your No mean No and your Yes mean Yes, "Power is not given to you. You have to take it." says Beyoncé Knowles. Know your worth and demand to be treated with dignity and respect by any and everyone no matter how big or small you are and no matter your circumstances or where you come from, or what you have been through, "Mistakes are a fact of life; it is the response to the error that counts" words from the beautiful poet Nikki Giovanni.

So know that in life you will make mistakes but those mistakes do not define you and that it doesn't mean your life is over because of them, Oprah Winfrey said, "Forget about the fast lane. If you really want to fly, just harness your power to your passion." With that said stay away from drugs they mean you no good, alcohol brings out the ugly truths and can put you in some dangerous situations I've learned this the hard way, Most importantly your vagina is your blessings, yes I said Vagina! And it is not a tool to use to get what you want, it needs to be treated with love dignity and respect so keep your legs closed until you understand the power of what you have between them, words by the famous actress Audrey Hepburn, "There is more to sex appeal than just measurements. I don't need a bedroom to prove my womanliness.

    I can convey just as much sex appeal, picking apples off a tree or standing in the rain." Know that there is more to life than being pretty, I tell my own daughter of how I knew a lot of girls that were pretty in high school that aren't so pretty now so don't get caught up on looks, know that boys want what you have so you don't need to chase them, or disrespect yourself in order to get them because truth is they will never respect you once you give it up. Erica Jong a famous author said, "You see a lot of smart guys with dumb women, but you hardly ever see a smart woman with a dumb Guy." These are words to remember and to live by.

    Be careful in how you dress yourself knowing the difference between classy and trashy will determine how boys treat you, "A girl should be two things: classy and fabulous." These are the famous words from Coco Chanel. So have pride in how you look and know that colorful hair and tattoo's, and having several piercings' may keep you from getting a good job or the respect that you're looking for. Respect each other don't hate on the next girl she is not you and you are not her, Please stop fighting one another and recording it for likes; if someone says or does something that you don't like try to just walk away, In the words of the late great singer Billie Holiday "sometimes it's worse to win a fight than to lose." Think about that statement the next time you engage in a fight, if you win what have you really won?

    Marian Wright Edelman who is an activist for Children's Rights said, "Don't feel entitled to anything you didn't sweat and struggle for." So don't depend on anybody to take care of you because they will do it in the ways that they see fit, Hey young girls in the words of Tyra Banks, "You have what it takes to be a victorious, independent, fearless woman." Try hard to think with your mind and not with your emotions, and forgive yourself you are only human; Oprah Winfrey said, "Doing the best at this moment puts you in the best place for the next moment."

    The best advice that I can give to all of you young girls in the world along with the quotes from all of the beautiful women that inspired me; is to put God first, pray to him and ask for guidance.

    Young girls if you understand and follow these steps in life it will help you along your journey to greatness. Hey young girls, the world is watching you because you are the future of this nation, so help set the standards for the younger girls coming up behind you. I am proud of you and wish you good luck!

    Hey Young Girls the world is yours!

Let's Pray

Hallelujah...hallelujah...hallelujah. Because of YOU JESUS, I am healed, because of YOU, I am standing, because of YOU, I am victorious, because of YOU, I have overcome. I will forever praise you. I will magnify your name. I will tell of your goodness. I will give you honor. I will give you praise. Just when I was about to give up and turn back you blessed me and now I am able to tell the world, I am blessed. Amen!

Index

Page

9   We Are Not Different………Charmaine Betty-Singleton

Used to Be Abused

12   Mended by His Grace……………………………………………Ariel Mitchell
15   The Stranger That I Know …………………………NaKyiah K. Nichols
18   No More Pain………………………………………………………Rene Michelle
21   Why I Stayed, Then I Ran ……………………………Torri Rodgers-Ball
24   Lost Thoughts……………………………………………………Tearra Walker
26   The Wrong Kind of Love………………………………Brittany Williams
32   Smiling Through My Pain …………………………Elizabeth Rowland
36   My Struggles to Survive……..…………………………Shanique Culler

I'm Not Perfect But I'm Worth It

41   She is Worth More……………………………………………………Carrie Shaw
42   I Am…………………………………………………………NaKyiah K. Nichols
43   Who Am I …………………………………………………………Carrie Shaw
45   For I Am Me……………………………………………………Shanique Culler
46   Letter to My Daughters…………………………Fisiwe Zwana Freeman
47   Pretty Little Thick Girl ……………………………NaKyiah K. Nichols
48   Who I Am Created to Be ………………………………………Carolyn Terry
49   You Are A Queen ……………………………………………………Raiya Coates
50   Spirit………………………………………………………NaKyiah K. Nichols
51   True Love Awaits ……………………………Lakita Stewart-Thompson
53   I am Destinee, Destiny is Me…………………………Destinee Thompson

Learning to Live Without You

58	It Didn't Break Me, Only Made Me Stronger	Carolyn Terry
64	Losing My Mother	Elisabeth Budd-Brown
66	My Heart in Human Form	NaKyiah K. Nichols
68	Losing My Heart, My Best Friend	Raven Cassidone
72	Truly His Mooky-Mook	NaKyiah K. Nichols
75	Strength By The Side of the Bed	Lolita Cleveland
78	My Enemy My Angel	Minister Tanya Baylor
84	Words of Encouragement	Raven Cassidone

It's Not Unto Death

88	I Can See	NaKyiah K. Nichols
89	Broken With Purpose	Monique "Poetic Rain "Favors
92	Born into a Life Sentence	Raven Cassidone
93	The Definition of My Sanity	Taylor Culmer
94	Believing is Not Always Seeing	Mindy Ellison

Let's Sex Talk About Sex

102	I Will Speak Up	Janie Williams Brown
103	No Means No But	Carolyn Terry
106	Royalty Lies With	Mishelle Mungin
107	The "Ugly" Duckling	Jo Shanique Henningham
110	My Brown Boy	Janie Williams Brown
111	Little Sister	Tia Parker
112	Just a Form Godliness	Charlene Nensala
114	Oh How I Wish	Minister Tanya Baylor
119	A Fool for Boo Boo	Lakita Stewart-Thompson
123	The Divine Gift	Torri Rodgers-Ball

Why Daddy

126	Me	Kalia Foster
128	Absent	NaKyiah K. Nichols
131	Filling the Void	Raiya Coates
133	A Yearning for You	Lakita Stewart-Thompson
135	Healing Is A Process	Kimberly Nicholson
138	My Cross	Monique "Poetic Rain" Favors

You're Expected to Win

143	Just Like a Lemon, I'm Being Squeezed	Charlene Nensala
145	My Mistakes Became My Testimony	LaShonda Alexis
149	Stand	Anoved Sivad
150	The Power of Influence	Shaneiqua L. Washington
153	What Lies Underneath	Charlene Nensala
155	Overcomer is My Name	Shalonda Treasure Williams
161	Where is the Love	Kalia Foster
163	Give it to Him	Anoved Sivad
164	Hey Young Girls the World is Yours	Monique Price

Resources

Abuse

Center for Healthy Maryland
Website: http://healthymaryland.org/public-health/domestic-violence/

Maryland Network against Domestic Violence
Website: http://mnadv.org/

House of Ruth, MD
Website: http://www.hruth.org/give-help.asp
Phone: 24 hour hotline 410-889-7884

An Abuse, Rape, and Domestic Violence Aid and Resource Collection
Website: http://www.aardvarc.org/dv/states/mddv.shtml
(relationship abuse, sexual victimization, stalking etc...)

Mignon Brown Anderson
Lakeisha Brown Foundation
Website: http://lakeishabrownfoundation.org
Phone: 202-710-7221
Email: Lakeishabrownfoundation24@gmail.com

Sexual Planning/Pornography/Addictions

Center of Disease Control and Prevention
Website: http://www.cdc.gov/teenpregnancy/parent-guardian-resources/index.htm

Planned Parenthood of Metropolitan Washington, DC, Inc.
Website: http://www.plannedparenthood.org/planned-parenthood-metropolitan-washington-dc

Address: 1108 16th Street, NW, Washington, DC 20036
Phone: 202-347-8500

Planned Parenthood of Maryland
http://www.plannedparenthood.org/planned-parenthood-maryland
Address: 330 N. Howard Street, Baltimore, MD 21201
Phone: 410- 576-1414

National Center on Domestic Violence and Sexual Violence
Website: http://www.ncdsv.org/ncd_linkschildsexabuse.html

Setting the Captives Free
Website: www.settingcaptivesfree.com

Christians in recovery
Website: christians-in-recovery.org

Healing for the Soul
Website: www.healingforthesoul.org

Counseling /Coaching Services

Dr. Kiu Eubanks, Ph.D
Guided Pathways Clinical Solutions, LLC
Website: http://www.gpsclinical.com/services.html
Address: 100 West Rd Suite 316, Towson, MD 21204
Phone: 443-200-4872
Email: info@gpsclinical.com

Latasha Matthews, LPC, CPCS
Illumination Counseling and Coaching, LLC
http://www.illuminationcc.com/
Address: 1840 Old Norcross Road, Suite 200, Lawrenceville, GA 30044
Phone: 678-585-1966
Email: latasha@illuminationcc.com

Gwendolyn Latrice Young
GLY Consulting
Website: http://glyconsulting.com/
Email: glyconsulting@gmail.com

Spiritual Guidance

Pastor Al Harris and Co-Pastor Sabrina Harris
Deliverance Headquarters for All People
Website: http://www.deliverance-hq.org/
Address: 11064 Livingston Road, Unit F, Fort Washington, MD 20744
Phone: 301-203-2534
Email: deliverance.headquarters@gmail.com

Jacqueline Barnes
Jacqueline Barnes Ministries
Website: http://www.jacquelinebarnesministries.com/
Phone: 708-859-1439
Email: jbarnes.info@gmail.com

Mental Health

National Alliance on Mental Illness (NAMI)
Website: www.nami.org
Phone: 800-950-6264 (helpline)

National Hopeline Network Crisis Hotline
Website: www.hopleline.com
Phone: 1-800-SUICIDE (784-2433)

National Suicide Prevention
Website: www.suicidepreventionlifeline.org
Phone: 1-800-273-TALK (8255)

Health Services

Capital Women's Care
Website: http://www.cwcare.net/
Phone: 301-340-8339

US Dept. of Health and Human Services
Website: http://www.hrsa.gov/womenshealth/
Phone: 877-464-4772

Support Services for women and girls
Gwendolyn L. Young
Jacqueline Barnes
Seed of Hope
Website: http://www.sowaseedofhope.org/
Email: customerservice@mysoh.org

Kashonna Holland
Simply Kashonna
Website: http://simplykashonna.com/
Address: P.O. Box 8570, Elkridge, MD
Phone: 443-983-5293
Email: info@simplykashonna.com

Charmaine Betty-Singleton
Praises to the King Enterprises, LLC
http://www.ptkenterprisesllc.com/
PO Box 57460
Webster, TX 77598
Phone: 1 - (281) - 900 - 0124
Fax: 1 - (800) - 705 - 5324
Email: ptkenterprisesllc@gmail.com

Lakita Stewart-Thompson
National Association of Mothers & Daughters United Worldwide
Website: http://www.namaduw.org/
Phone: 202-618-9673
Email: namaduworldwide@yahoo.com

About the Lead Author

NaKyiah K. Nichols is a youth dedicated to ministering the word of GOD through Mime. While in her mother's womb NaKyiah was anointed through various words of prophesy spoken into her life. GOD has used her to minister healing encouragement, and deliverance into the lives of his people. NaKyiah is a member of the chosen generation that has said, **"Here I am LORD send me."**

NaKyiah is a 13 year old, 8th grade honor roll and National Junior Honor Society student in Charles County, MD. Under the spiritual guidance of Pastor Al Harris and Co-Pastor Rev. Sabrina Harris of Deliverance Headquarters for All People in Ft. Washington, MD; NaKyiah is actively involved in ministry, and serving as a youth missionary.

NaKyiah has ministered at various churches, conferences, community outreach programs, youth revivals, funerals, retirement, baby showers and birthday celebrations etc. NaKyiah was privilege to have the opportunity to minister in the presence of the Maryland State Lt. Governor Anthony Brown, the Baltimore Ravens Chaplin, Pastor Rod Hairston, Philadelphia Eagles retired running back Mr. Brian Westbrook and former NY Jets wide receiver Mr. Tavon Mason.

She also gave a stellar performance in the Washington DC 21st century program in their renditions of The Wiz, The Lion King and Howard Road Island.

In 2013, at the age of 11 NaKyiah was afforded the opportunity to be a guest teacher and speaker at a dance conference to attendees from age 5 to adult leaders within the churches and community in Prince Fredrick Maryland.

In alignment with her gifting NaKyiah declared at a young age that her favorite scripture is, 1st Corinthians 10:13. NaKyiah possesses a love for GOD and his people!

For Booking,
Email: nakyiah.k.nichols@gmail.com
Connect: https://www.facebook.com/pages/NaKyiah-K-Nichols-Anointed-Mime-Dancer/485353944816827

Reflections

Reflections

Reflections

About Through Words Publishing, LLC

For writers/authors:
Find out how to publish your next book with
Through Words Publishing, LLC

For readers:
Get access to published books at
www.Amazon.com
Visit: www. Namaduw.org

"We Change Lives through Words"

Email us your story:
momentsinherstory@gmail.com

www.ingramcontent.com/pod-product-compliance
Lightning Source LLC
LaVergne TN
LVHW051120080426
835510LV00018B/2152